Dinner Survival

Cooking for the Rushed

Sandi Richard

Scribner

New York London Toronto Sydney

SCRIBNER
A Division of Simon & Schuster, Inc.
1230 Avenue of the Americas
New York, NY 10020

First Scribner trade paperback edition January 2009

SCRIBNER and design are registered trademarks of The Gale Group, Inc.,
used under license by Simon & Schuster, Inc., the publisher of this work.

COOKING FOR THE RUSHED, DINNER SURVIVAL, THE FAMILY DINNER FIX,
THE HEALTHY FAMILY, GETTING YA THROUGH THE SUMMER and LIFE'S ON FIRE
are trademarks of Cooking for the Rushed, Inc.

For information about special discounts for bulk purchases, please contact Simon & Schuster Special Sales
at 1-800-456-6798 or business@simonandschuster.com.

Designed by Cooking for the Rushed, Inc.
Manufactured in the United States of America

10 9 8 7 6 5 4 3 2 1

ISBN-13: 978-1-4165-4364-0
ISBN-10: 1-4165-4364-3

Also by Sandi Richard
The Family Dinner Fix
The Healthy Family
Life's on Fire
Getting Ya Through the Summer

To our readers and to our readers with diabetes
Dinner Survival: Cooking for the Rushed is not a cookbook which claims to cater to the complex dietary needs of
a person with diabetes. The nature of this book is speed and nutrition. A large number of North Americans have some
form of diabetes; therefore we feel it is helpful to provide information on food exchanges and food group values.

In view of the complex nature of health in relation to food and activity, this book is not intended to replace professional or
medical advice. The author and publisher expressly disclaim any responsibility for any liability, loss or risk, personal or otherwise, which is incurred as a consequence, directly or indirectly, of the use and application of any of the contents of this book.

This book is dedicated to

The Family

Table of Contents

Meal Plans

Red:	Not-So-Chili Pasta with Broccoli (Bow Ties and Trees)
Green:	Baked Potato & Cheddar Soup with Dinner Rolls and Salad
Red:	Ginger-Lime Chicken with Rice, Zucchini and Mushrooms
Yellow:	Oven Pork Roast with Applesauce, Baby Potatoes, Gravy and Asparagus
Blue:	Salsa-Cinnamon Chicken with Couscous, Peas and Corn

Green:	Spiced Cheddar Burgers with Cold Veggies and Dip
Blue:	Spinach & Cheese–Stuffed Pasta Shells with Caesar Salad
Red:	Sweet & Sour Chicken with Rice and Baby Carrots
Yellow:	Steak with Red Wine Gravy, Crinkle Fries and Roasted Parm Asparagus
Red:	Udon Noodle Soup with Crunchy Spinach Salad

Table of Contents

Table of Contents

Introduction

Are we neglecting the most influential purchasing group in society?

"The Family"

If all families banded together they would be the most influential voice to change the eating habits of North America. Yet in many ways, both in the food business and in education, it's the most neglected group when it comes to catering to their health. Fad diets and their exercise programs usually don't include living life in the 21st century!

We (as a society) tell parents they should set aside time to cook a great dinner for their family each night. This should include more fish, more beans and lentils and more veggies. We also tell them to make sure they set aside time to eat together, to connect.

We tell parents, "Get your kids active. Keep their minds occupied with good activities so the kids don't go astray!"

We show parents and kids all the cool stuff they should have (through TV, magazines, books and so on). Parents want their kids to have all the cool stuff the other kids have: the digital box, the TVs and the iPods, so parents work longer hours.

We tell parents that they need to set quiet time aside in their day for themselves to regenerate and to function properly. Studies show that they should get 8 hours of sleep a night, no less than 7.

We tell parents to be a good example to their children, by instilling discipline and activity into their own lives, so their children can live by example.

We tell parents that having regular dates with their partners and being intimate at least a couple of times per week will ensure that the relationship stands on a solid foundation.

Are you tired yet? Let's do the math!

Parents work longer to get their kids stuff:

1 hour drive to work **+ 8 hours** work **+ 1 hour** drive home **= 10 hours total**

Parents rush home in a panic to get kids to activities which will keep their minds and bodies healthy:

15 to 45 minutes driving kids to activity (let's take an average **30 minutes** each way) **+** length of activity 1 to 3 hours…let's take an average of **2 hours = 3 hours total**

…turn the page for more math

Introduction...(cont.)

Parents make a healthy dinner for their kids: take out ingredients and equipment, prep, cook, clean up, eat, and get changed and organized to drive kids and so on.

30 to 60 minutes to take out stuff, prep and cook (let's say **45 minutes) + 15 minutes** to clean up **+ 30 minutes** to eat **+ 15 minutes** to get changed **= 1 hour and 45 minutes total**

Now add **8 hours** to sleep and get ready in the morning into this equation. Let's do the math to see what's left in the day.

24 hours - 10 (work) - 3 (driving) - 1.75 (prepping, making, eating, then cleaning up dinner) - 8 (sleep) = 1 hour and 15 minutes
to split up the things you have left to do. "Well, I have too much to do in 1 hour and 15 minutes! What should I give up?" you ask...the sleep, the intimacy, the quiet time, the exercise...gee and then there are the forms to fill out for the kids' activities, homework corrections, the book I want to read to my kids at bedtime, the phone call I never made to my best friend or my brother, my sister, my mom...the laundry, grocery shopping...

Now just for the fun of it, let's plunk in a fad diet, or shall we call it "A New Lifestyle"? (Like giving it a new name changes anything!)

Are parents getting it all done? Suuuure they are!...NO they aren't! Most are plunking down on a sofa in sheer exhaustion, flipping the channels for any news show that won't tell them how inactive or obese they are! (...and hoping the popcorn is low fat!) They are getting divorced and eating out! They are exhausted, broke, insecure, feel guilty, feel alone, and feel like failures that can never seem to do it right or catch up. And the bonus for most—they're overweight! Great!

We hold the parent up high, with accolades, telling them they have the most important job on earth, but we lambaste them with unrealistic expectations of what it takes to be a great parent. Parents can't keep up with this pace, but we stand by and watch the entire western culture crumble in despair.

Well, you say, I'm single, so how does this affect me? Oh my lovey dovey...it does! You see, companies cater to the group that will make them the most money. So, if companies need to cater to **The Family** because it's the largest, most influential group with the greatest buying power, they are going to give the family what the family desperately needs. Time! Food companies are in a constant search for something that will be quick and easy, something that will save us time. Whom are they catering to? They can supply larger quantities of not-so-healthy food to the families who are buying them. The family buys that food with a hope and a prayer that it will give them more time. The law of supply and demand, sweet pea, is why many healthier foods are so darned expensive. That affects us all, including you!

If we can help **The Family** navigate their way through this chaos, I'm telling you, it will change everything for everyone. It can certainly change what's on TV, it can change what fast food restaurants serve, it can change how families spend time together, and it can change the yardstick to measure what's normal.

Is Guilt from the Lack of Time Keeping the Family from Optimum Health?

Have you ever noticed what's on the way to the grocery store? A parent is missing a grocery item to complete dinner (that's 'cause they didn't meal plan; we'll talk about that later). They get in their car to pick up the missing item, guess what they need to cope with all the way to the grocery store…yup, the picture says it all!

If a mom opts for fast food in the midst of her hectic day, deep down inside her soul, there are so many emotions attached to that decision. Guilt for spending the money, guilt for feeding her family something that may not be as healthy for them as she would like, guilt for not having the traditional "sit down at the dinner table" meal that she envisioned before she became a mom. But if she doesn't opt for it, she feels guilty because she may not have had time to get a decent meal on the table, guilty that she hasn't had time to spend with her kids, helping with homework, reading and so on.

I may be using a woman as an example, but in no way am I excluding dads from this scenario. Some of today's dads are just as involved, if not more so, than moms. My oldest son is a prime example. He was the primary care giver of Aly, our granddaughter, while his wife was finishing her degree and establishing her career. (And what a fine job he did with that perfect and overly gifted girl! No bias here!)

Unlike a few generations ago, a mom or dad in today's family feels the pressure to be all and have it all. I remember when I felt like I didn't have it together when it came to making dinner. It affected every area of my life. I felt guilty about everything. I remember trying to talk to women about it back then, but rarely would I find someone who wanted to admit that they too weren't pulling it off. In turn they would make themselves feel better by not telling the whole truth. I would walk away feeling more like a failure than when I began to share. I stopped sharing!

**I believe one of the most damaging things parents can do
to themselves, to others and to the growth of our nation's children
is avoid sharing with other parents the truth about our parenting struggles.**

It has been said it takes a village to raise a child. I believe that means everyone has different talents and different points of view and we must share them with each other. By pooling our resources together, the child will be more likely to make it in this world.

Back on the farm, Aunt Bee and Uncle Ernie would tell the truth. While chopping wood, Uncle Ernie would tell the young dad that it's normal for sex to get sparser once the responsibility of children is the dominating factor in the marriage.

While making dinner or canning, Aunt Bee would share stories to help the young mom understand that strains in the marriage are normal and often due to current circumstances. The young couple would return after a hard day of labor with a different point of view, a new understanding of each other and of marriage and a stronger bond with family. Advice came from trusted adults other than your parents. Family and friends weren't competing with you, they were watching over you. Elders would pass on much needed advice to the younger generation, and society was just a little more balanced because most parents were on the same playing field.

Notice what has drastically changed today…families don't work together anymore. Nowadays, stay-at-home parents feel a bit guilty that their children don't have the same financial advantage as some of their friends who have parents who work outside of the home. The parents who work outside of the home feel guilty that their children don't enjoy the same time advantage as their friends with stay-at-home parents. Every family in the neighborhood will have a completely different situation. So you see the day-to-day parental playing field has drastically changed in a very short period of time in history. Because of this, today's parents feel like they are constantly competing with their peers and with the previous generation. This has led to a society that is out of balance and guilt ridden.

It drives me bonkers when one mom says to another, "Oooh, I just never had any problems with my kids." Well, I could say that too, now that I am not in the thick of a teen's attitude, or a terrible two who just threw up on the floor after a temper tantrum. Or now that I am not trying to get one kid with a fever to the doctor, just when the other desperately needs a nap! Our kids are amazing. We adore them. They are the most beautiful people I have ever met…NOW!

So, back to food and why I believe it's all of these other outside forces that screw up dinner rather than the food itself. Dinner is just one more thing on the long list of things a parent needs to fix. Dinner is bigger than food. It's about our emotions, our health and bonding with our families. We can choose from our long lists of priorities, but we need to feed our families, so we can't omit dinner!

Remember our time equation…I hope we are all smart enough to figure out that 1 hour and 15 minutes is not enough time to accomplish everything we need to do, so some will do dinner, some will do take-out, some will read to their kids and some will do laundry. We all have different coping mechanisms and we all have a different idea of what will keep our family balanced, focused and healthy.

Even the Bathroom Isn't Sacred

If you are a parent you are all too familiar with this scene. As soon as you need to go to the bathroom, it's like the world needs you. My best friend, Glennie (who wishes not to be mentioned), says that it's like our butts have sonar. The minute our trousers are dropped and our butt is in close proximity to the toilet seat, the kids know. They just know!

The phone must also have a silent shrill which affects kid's ears, like a dog whistle does to dogs, especially if you work from home! I remember saying my kids had a rare disease called telephonitis. Every bang, fall and temper tantrum my children ever had happened the minute I picked up the phone. If it was an important business call, the elevation of their voices increased by at least two decibels.

Time is a rare commodity for all of us, but for parents especially. We tell parents that it's so important to put some of their needs ahead of their children. Many books use the airplane oxygen mask as an example. The airlines say to put your own mask on first so that you are more equipped to handle helping your children. That's all good and I believe it's a good analogy. I am a firm believer that if we have a little time alone to read, exercise or be with a friend, the recharge will feel like we have more time, not less. But…

There's one little glitch with families…When so many things feel like emergencies and parents have 1 hour and 15 minutes left to do everything other than work, travel and activities, what should they do in that whole 15 seconds when they should put themselves first? You get the point.

According to all the books, we are supposed to be mentally, spiritually, emotionally and physically balanced. FOR FAMILIES, WHEN? In no way am I saying this can't be turned around or that parents need to be fed pablum. Not at all. I am just saying that from my many observations dealing with families for years, they all *want* to be balanced, but they're not. Each family thinks they are the ONLY ones who are out of balance.

So how did we get here? We've tried everything. We even fought for more time. Remember when the stores were closed on Sundays? I know we live in a democratic country, which I am very proud of, and that everyone doesn't worship on Sunday. I just can't help but wonder if, in our pursuit to be more constitutionally correct and get more time to shop, we actually lost the battle we won. Think about it; no matter what our race or religious beliefs, in the pursuit of time, we fought to have the one day we could count on for rest taken away. It's gone, gone forever! There were no sports on Sunday. We went to church; my mom prepared the weekly roast beef or turkey dinner. (And on Mondays we always had leftover hot beef or turkey sandwiches…yum!) Mom had time to breathe, to make dinner; every kid we knew was doing what we were doing, eating Sunday dinner with family. It wasn't an option to miss it! The last generations figured some stuff out! Think about it…Sunday dinner, then the most hectic day following…leftovers!

Sundays have become one of the busiest days of the week for most parents. Why? Sports! Yup, we are trying to keep our kids healthy, keeping their brains active, so we put up with games, practices, fundraising meetings, you name it, on Sunday. I remember my pastor saying, "Satan sure is crafty; he used sports to keep us away from God and God's clear instruction to get rest on Sunday!" Now that I think about it, I've never read, "God created the world, and on the seventh day he answered all his e-mail, went to baseball practice, and went shopping!" That would just be weird!

So why don't families speak up, say no and insist on one day's rest to be with family? 'Cause we don't want to feel stupid in front of the other parents who will make fun of us. Maybe there are enough of us who feel the same way and we just don't know it! There are countless athletes from years past who went to church on Sunday, got to play with their friends and have a family dinner and became superstars despite it all.

If you have traveled to Europe, you know that in some places when the stores shut down after lunch, they aren't going to open up. That rest time is just too important to them. They need to recharge and it's not in their culture to care if that's not important to you. It's their philosophy as a group. They work around it. If you are a tourist, chances are your travel agent has prepared you for it, so you plan around it! What do you do in those two hours? Chances are you rest, just like they do!

Technology—The Good and the Bad

I believe parents also struggle, on top of everything else, with how to handle technology, TV and the internet. Most of us are connected to a computer all day, or at least a big part of the day, for our work. I love technology. I find it fascinating and helpful. If it wasn't for spell-check, grade school teachers of mine would still be shaking their heads over my spelling! But with the good comes the bad.

Is technology taking control of our homes? It's my humble opinion that it is. I also believe that if we don't control the use of technology in our homes, it can disconnect **The Family** like never before in history. We don't talk because we don't have to. One person's got earphones on listening to their favorite music, someone's watching TV in the living room and one parent is on the computer finishing up the demands of work! Did you say the demands of work? Yup, because of technology we are bringing the office home! Parents fake themselves out by thinking that if they take work home, they will have more time with their family.

Many companies have caught on to this and use it to perpetuate fear in their employees. "If you won't finish the work, the other guy will." Otherwise known as the "You can be replaced" blackmail...I, I, I, mean technique! Many parents stay in deadbeat jobs because they hold on to that fear of not being able to provide for their families.

A couple of years back I was invited to have a meeting with an executive from a large oil firm. They wanted to pilot a program for their employees that incorporated overall health both at work and home. Of course I was impressed with them and thrilled that our books were being considered as one of the tools. However, a story that exec shared with me that day was really the reason I was meant to be at that meeting.

When I asked her why her company had made this bold move, she explained. There is a large Swedish firm which is respected worldwide for its productivity. Her oil firm recently invited the leaders of this Swedish company to assist them so that they too could be more productive. The oil firm's execs escorted the Swedish company's execs through their offices and procedures. After 5:00 p.m. one of the Swedes asked, "Why are so many of your staff still here?" They replied that they likely didn't get their work done. The Swede asked, "Why?" The execs thought that was a peculiar question! The Swede continued, "And why do you allow them to stay late?" The oil execs were shocked! To make a long story short, the Swedes concluded that the biggest block in this oil company's work productivity was that there were too many meetings, which inhibited the employees from getting their work done. This led the staff to work longer, which kept them from having dinner with their families, which kept them from recharging so that they couldn't be as productive in between too many meetings the following day. WOW! Oh and by the way, the Swedish company's sick leave was almost nonexistent! What a shock!

Time Is on Your Side

Maybe in the previous story and in the following story lie some of the answers to get family health back on track:

A couple of years ago Ron and I took our first big trip alone, just the two of us, for six weeks, visiting four countries. We didn't bring computers, day timers, or business phone numbers, just a backpack and a carry-on for each of us. We were in the midst of filming our Food Network show, but prior to signing our contract, we all agreed that we would not be able to film during the time we had booked our trip. The production company had one year's notice. As the time grew closer they started back-pedaling. Fear was flooding our thoughts. We were scrambling to leave instructions for our assistant. We left additional pages for our son and daughter. (They would stay at the house and manage a few things while we were gone.) After all…the business could fall to pieces without someone managing every detail, every minute, of every day, couldn't it? Maybe Food Network would find someone prettier, younger, better. We had never left our work for more than one week! Despite all our fears, we left exactly as planned.

The business went along with its normal flow; people accepted that we were not returning until a certain date (and yes, we were buried with work when we got back). Only one person, outside the production company, got angry that we didn't have internet access where we were, and only one person phoned us outside of family. (A newspaper editor, Daryl, wanted to congratulate me on winning a Host of the Year award while away.)

Aaand my point is? After all that senseless worrying before we left, everything was intact and back to normal within days of our return…or was it? Nope, it wasn't…We were different! We were calmer, more focused, more balanced, more in love than the first day we laid eyes on each other. We were smarter, had a deeper connection with God, with each other, with our children and with the world. For six whole weeks there were no "I need it yesterday" phone calls, no meetings and no computers (other than the odd internet café to update the kids). We woke up, stared at the ocean, drank coffee, walked, hugged, ate interesting food…and, well, you know!!! (And that's only because we had more than 1 hour and 15 minutes to do everything.)

How Convenient Is Too Convenient?

Have you ever been really mad when you couldn't find the remote for the TV? I call it remote rage! Yup, I shamefully admit I've been there! I have spent 10-30 minutes looking angrily for a remote, so that I can save time flicking channels in the 1 hour and 15 minutes I have left to do everything else in my life. I'm telling you, we are out of control! Watch kids when they can't find the remote. They look for about two seconds, and if they can't find it they simply change the channels by hand.

Ponder the following…We read books that tell us how to diet when we get fed up about how we feel or what we look like. (After all, somebody at work said his diet plan was great!) We get on the bandwagon and get to the gym. We drink the water and eat the whatever-that-food-diet-says-works food! We call our friends…"Hey Joe, I just lost 3 inches off my waist 'cause of this fantastic newfangled book." Joe says, "Hey, thanks Frank," and goes out and buys the book, and he tells two friends, and so on and so on. (In the meantime Frank and Joe use a remote! They also ride the elevator, take the escalator and, for goodness' sake, don't even have to manually open a door or turn on a tap to wash their hands! We are far less active in our day-to-day tasks!)

Before you know it, Frank has to make his own whatever-that-diet-says-works food, because his family is fed up with his weird food. His wife is mostly fed up because she was having a hard enough time making one meal, let alone two, in the 1 hour and 15 minutes she has to do everything else. Now she feels bad because she wants to support him and is proud of him. But that's not how he's reading it. He gradually loses steam and because he can't keep up, off the diet he goes. Is this good for **The Family**?

Will the Real Family Please Stand Up?

OK, so we use remotes and we don't have to open doors. Everything around us is convenient and either done for us or just about! As a meal planner, the topic of convenient food baffles me more than any other topic when it comes to **The Family**.

The following scenario I'm about to describe hasn't happened once or twice; it's the norm.

Sally, her husband John and their two children have been chosen to be a family I will help on my television show, *Fixing Dinner*. I get a feeling of their routines and their challenges and gather the recipes that their family is familiar with. I ask the parents to tell me which kid hates which food. I now want to know which meals are hassle-free…the meals everyone likes! I remove the parents, for a bit, so that I can use pictures of recipes to find out what the kids find appealing to look at and what they may try. The kids swoon over certain pictures and they say things like, "I love chicken," or, "Yum! Peppers, especially the red ones." I go back to the list of what the parent says the child hates. Yup, red peppers and chicken are on the list.

I have sticky notes on all the pages the kids pick out. I show them to the parents and they are shocked and amazed. They say things like, "Joooohnny, you have to be honest with Sandi!" When it's implied that Johnny isn't being honest, Johnny starts to second guess his decision.

I explain to Sally and her husband that children, like adults, eat with their eyes and that I use the pictures as a tool to find out what is real and what is not. The parents glance at the recipe beside the photo and say things like, "Oh, we never use canned soup. There's a ton of sodium in that." "I see this recipe uses ketchup; it's packed with sugar, isn't it?" "I can't afford to use boneless, skinless chicken, I have to bone it myself." And so on.

MOM, CLICK ON THE DOUBLE CHEESE BURGER… I'm STARVING!

I ask the parents, with the children present, how many times they eat out in the week (the answer is always) "…Ooooh almost never!" (Sure, that's why a fast food joint goes up on every corner every minute of the day…because no one eats there!) At that point I get tough. I ask, if there isn't a problem, why are they on the show? I tell them the average family eats out 3-4 times weekly. I ask them to trace their tracks in the past week. With all family members present it becomes clear that in fact, like many other families, they eat out more than they thought. They begin to crumble and even admit they have their favorite take-out places on speed dial or on their computers.

They freak out when I ask to see their pantry. I find packaged cookies, treats, chips and soda pop. The freezer is full of pizza, pastries, premade hamburgers, flash frozen chicken breasts, bags of chicken fingers. Remember their concern with sugar in ketchup and salt in soup? Sally and her husband are embarrassed. Their embarrassment changes to joy when I explain they are just like everyone else and that it's their perception of convenience that formed their bad habits. I explain that if I can help them change their perception of convenience, their habits will turn healthy. They're excited!

You see, I believe this:

> **The Family tries to do everything right and know everything they should know, but they don't have time to get all the information they need in the 1 hour and 15 minutes they have to do everything else.**

Cause-and-effect is that people get bits and pieces of information from doctors, medical professionals, TV shows, books, magazines and their friends who all have the right answers. Preservative-free, organic, sugar-free, no salt, no chicken, no beef, no dairy, no bread…depending who's talking. People flip around like fish out of water trying to sift through a sea of information. In the meantime, people need to realize that unless a point of view includes family life, those narrow-minded opinions are actually assisting in the disappearance of the family dinner. Until we recognize that food information is useless unless it allows for the realities of family life, things will get worse before they get better. Can't anyone see this?

> **I'm telling you, "Dinner is bigger than food!"**

There are a lot of hurting families out there. Do you know what happens with the families I work with on my television show from the beginning to the end? They stop blaming each other! They take turns; we make the food match their schedules. Parents are in shock that a teen loves to cook. A husband or wife is in shock that either doesn't work late to avoid dinner. They start to drop some of the less important activities. They opt for the convenience of having a butcher take the bones and skin off their chicken and opt out of buying junk food full of empty calories. It's quite amazing!

Going back to one of my opening phrases: If the population would band together and recognize that **The Family** is the most influential buying group in the country, all of us would be able to take advantage of less expensive healthy food all the time. Plain and simple, it's the law of supply and demand!

So let's get started.

First, I want you to understand,

> **"What you do when you walk in the door at dinner time does matter."**

**If you incorporate these few simple habits on the next two pages,
you will notice dinner-making will seem much more peaceful, immediately!**

Don't Change Yet!

Why do I always start a recipe with the above words?

These are the most important instructions on your recipe! Really!! We get home, we take off our coat, climb into something comfy…NOOOOOOOOOO!!!!! I swear there is a direct relationship between wearing comfy clothing and not cooking dinner. Why? Because as soon as our minds have said work is officially over, we don't want to work anymore.

Work is not over until work is over!

So a few extra minutes of work and an adjustment in mindset will change my eating life?
YEEEEEEEEEEES!!!!

Take your coat or jacket off and immediately put a long apron on, over your work clothes (this is for you too, guys), take out your ingredients and take out the equipment you will use to make the meal. You have now committed to making dinner. If you really don't trust yourself to cook, look for things in the recipe that would be helpful to get you started. For example, if there are sautéed onions in the recipe, I may cut the onion first, let it gently sauté and then take the rest of my ingredients out along with the equipment; then I have doubly committed.

Just like exercise, the problem with dinner lies in getting started. So please…buy a long apron if you don't have one. If you do have one, keep it close by. This is a discipline that will become a habit. The habit of making dinner is good!

Why do I ask you to purchase a separate timer than what is on your stove or microwave?

Almost all of the families I work with initially think this is the dumbest thing they have ever heard. Yet, all the families now find it their most valuable tool.

This timer is to time **you**, not the food! It is to set a boundary around you and the family until the job is done. It is to remind you that the task is short, not long. It makes you boogie!

Your stuff is all out, your equipment is all out and now you have set a boundary around yourself to get the job done! If your partner wants to ask you a question, point to the timer; it's the timer's fault, not yours. If the phone rings, you can call whomever back as soon as the timer rings. If one of the kids is hanging on your leg in a fit of anger, drag them along with you; they soon learn: the timer is on and I get ALL of Mom or Dad after the timer rings. Will you always beat the timer before it rings? No, but that's not the point. You will almost always beat it, IF you have taken out all your ingredients and equipment first.

A mentor of mine, Jim Rohn, has a saying, "Don't work while you play and don't play while you work." I believe this is a significant statement for busy parents today. If you are playing while you work, you can't give 100% to your work. If you are working while you play, the family feels like you are not giving them 100% of you. So, don't look at the timer as ignoring the needs of your family, look at it as a great habit. They would rather have all of you once you're done than a frustrated half of you while you're trying to juggle two things at once!

Why do I say it's essential to take your recipe out the night before?

If you think this little habit is insignificant, just try it for a few days. You'll be so frustrated with yourself afterward if you forget. By glancing at your recipe the night before you do several things. You will end up taking out something to defrost if need be. You may realize that the following day's time crunch changed, so while you are folding laundry or in-between helping with homework or watching your favorite weekly show, it may take a lot of pressure off your back to prep just one thing.

What makes my meal planning strategy different and stick-to-it-able?

We always hear that meal planning is essential, but we don't learn how to do it. Our mother's mother's way isn't going to fly today because that requires you to repeat the work weekly. In the 1 hour and 15 minutes we have to do everything else in our life…yeah…I don't think so!

My strategy develops a plan your family buys into.

Your family buys into the plan because they help create it!

The written plan you create together is used over and over.

You never have to do the work again.

I suggest you get your family involved in the process for three weeks. (That's how long most diets last!) Then you have three physical plans to work with. If your family is happy with repeating those three weeks forever, your work is done forever. If the family wants a new week in the rotation, add a week at a time, whenever you want. You always have the previous written meal plans to work with in the meantime.

Meal Planning for the 21st Century

If you know you are having cheesy lasagna for dinner, will you eat that same thing for lunch? Not likely. So, instinctively you will choose something different. When something is different, it starts to balance your diet naturally; it becomes a habit and your body starts to change.

Once your body starts to change and you have more energy, the family will be more at peace; that's the time to make little changes in activity. I tell you, this is not only doable and sustainable, it's the miracle pill everyone's looking for! Why? Because it's convenient!

Diets, for the most part, are only sustainable for a few weeks because diets are not convenient. They do not incorporate life's busyness! When people cannot sustain a diet, they beat themselves up and feel like a failure. By contrast, repeat this meal planning exercise for just a few weeks and life actually gets easier. This is because you now have three weeks of master grocery lists that your family has created. You feel like a winner!

Five Basic Steps to Change Dinner Time Forever

1. Create a blank grocery list and tack it in a central location in the kitchen. Use our grocery lists in this book as an example of how to set it up or just print a blank grocery list from **www.cookingfortherushed.com**.
Tell your family members to give you dinner suggestions for meals they will actually eat. You will likely need to ask over and over again and, if necessary, threaten to make all the suggestions yourself.

2. Write down the meals and which recipe book they can be found in. Make sure the five meals are not all the same. You need a variety of meals to keep your week nutritionally balanced! If two people have chosen something similar you may have to ask someone to change their first pick, promising to transfer that meal to the following week.

3.   Create your master shopping list. (The list which will NEVER need to be done again! Crazy, you say? You won't know unless you DO IT!) The asker of the meals pours a cup of tea, finds the five recipes the family has chosen and transfers every single ingredient from each recipe to the master list. DO NOT LEAVE INGREDIENTS OFF THE LIST IF YOU HAVE THEM IN THE HOUSE. THIS IS YOUR MASTER LIST, NOT THE LIST YOU WILL TAKE TO THE STORE. Write the ingredients under each category according to where you will find those items at your particular grocery store. Don't forget to include ingredients you serve with the main course.

Put your master list in a plastic sheet protector and put that in a small binder close to your recipe books. Show EVERYONE where it is.

4.   Check which groceries you will need to purchase to complete your week of meals, using your master list. This is a perfect job for the asker of the meals to delegate.

The beauty of the master list is that it is so complete that anyone in your home can create a shopping list for ingredients that need to be purchased at the grocery store to complete that week any time in the future! Our readers tell us they create their shopping lists from the master list in different ways. Some use a washable marker on the plastic sheet protector to cross off items they don't need to purchase. Some use a separate piece of paper to jot down the items they need. Some photocopy their master list and cross off items directly on the photocopy. Don't forget to add the other things you will need at the store, like toilet paper and lunch box items.

5.   Go buy your groceries. Then, every night at dinner discuss which meal fits your schedule for the following night.

Each week you follow these steps you will have a new meal plan to add to your book.

On the weeks you don't have time use one that's already done.

Adjusting Nutritional Data
to Your Specific Needs

Before we get to the fun stuff in the upcoming pages, we need to deal with a few boring details. It's only two pages and you don't need to read them like the rest of the book, but you do want to tag them so they are readily available for easy reference.

- Most of the recipes in *Dinner Survival* provide 4-6 servings.
- Our test families varied in size. Some families said there was too much food for 4 people, and others thought it was just right.
- If you have 4 adults in your home with very healthy appetites the meal will probably serve 4 (when we write *Serves 4-6*). Sometimes someone gets a leftover lunch the next day!
- If you have younger children the recipe will probably serve 6 (when we write *Serves 4-6*).
- When a range is given for the number of servings a meal makes, the higher number is used. (i.e. when a meal says 4-6 servings, the nutritional data assumes you are dividing every component of the entire meal into 6 portions. The nutritional data is for one portion of each component. This also applies to the food exchange and food group data.)
Use the formula below to adjust the nutritional data when we write "Serves 4-6" and for your family it serves 4.

Adjusting Data When a Meal Serves 4 Instead of 6

# of g fat x 1.5 = # of g fat
i.e. 12 g fat x 1.5 = 18 g fat
(12 g fat per serving for 6 servings) = (18 g fat per serving for 4 servings)

This formula works for all our nutritional data.

Weights and Measures

- Imperial and Metric conversions are approximate only.
- Occasionally we do not provide exact conversions so readers can identify with the can, jar and package sizes produced in their country.
- When weights or measures are provided in both Imperial and Metric, nutritional data is calculated using the Imperial measure.
- When a range is given for a measure, the first given is used to calculate nutritional data.
- When a choice of two ingredients is listed (i.e. chicken or pork), the first ingredient is used for nutritional data.
- Ingredients listed as "optional" are not included in nutritional data.
- Fresh garlic (from a jar) is packed in citric acid (not oil).
- Vegetables and fruits are medium-size unless otherwise specified.
- Buns are 2 1/2 oz (or 70 g) and dinner rolls are 1 1/2 oz (or 42 g).

Conversion Charts

All measures are not the same.
These are a great guide—variances are minimal.

Liquid Measure

1 oz	30 ml
2 oz	60 ml
3 oz	100 ml
4 oz	125 ml
5 oz	150 ml
6 oz	190 ml
8 oz	250 ml
10 oz (1/2 pint)	300 ml
16 oz (1/2 liter)	500 ml
20 oz (1 pint)	600 ml
1 3/4 pints (1 liter)	1000 ml

Dry Measure

	stand	exact
1 oz	30 g	(28.3)
4 oz (1/4 lb)	125 g	(113.4)
8 oz (1/2 lb)	250 g	(226.8)
12 oz (3/4 lb)	375 g	
16 oz (1 lb)	500 g	
32 oz (2 lbs)	1 kg	

Can and Jar Comparison

4.5 oz	127 ml
8 oz	227 ml
10 oz	284 ml
12 oz	341 ml
14 oz	398 ml
19 oz	540 ml
24.5 oz	700 ml

Oven Temperatures

	F	C		F	C	
	175 -	80		350 -	175	
	200 -	95		375 -	190	
	225 -	110		400 -	205	mod hot
very slow	250 -	120		425 -	220	
	275 -	140		450 -	230	hot
slow	300 -	150		475 -	240	
mod slow	325 -	160		500 -	260	very hot

Buying Meat or Produce

1/2 lb	225 g
1 lb	450 g
1 1/2 lbs	675 g
2 lbs	900 g
2 1/2 lbs	1125 g
3 lbs	1350 g

Measuring

	stand	exact
1/4 tsp	1.2 ml	
1/2 tsp	2.4 ml	
1 tsp	5 ml	(4.7)
1 Tbsp (3 tsp)	15 ml	(14.2)
1/4 cup (4 Tbsp)	55 ml	(56.8)
1/3 cup	75 ml	(75.6)
1/2 cup	125 ml	(113.7)
2/3 cup	150 ml	(151.2)
3/4 cup	175 ml	(170)
1 cup	250 ml	(227.3)
4 1/2 cups	1 liter	(1022.9)

Monitoring Your Fat (for the day)

Percent	If You Eat...	Your Daily Fat Intake Should Be
	1500 calories	50 grams
	2000 calories	67 grams
30%	2500 calories	83 grams
	3000 calories	100 grams
	1500 calories	42 grams
	2000 calories	56 grams
25%	2500 calories	69 grams
	3000 calories	83 grams
	1500 calories	33 grams
	2000 calories	44 grams
20%	2500 calories	56 grams
	3000 calories	67 grams

Diabetic Food Exchanges and Food Choices

A very large number of people have some form of diabetes, so we feel it is important to include this information as well as the detailed nutritional analysis. Our recipes have very high standards for taste, speed and nutrition. It seems only fair to allow a person with diabetes the luxury of being able to use a regular cookbook with great-tasting meals. They can simply adjust components according to their specific dietary requirements. There is another very important reason for having food exchanges or choices. Some people use food exchanges or choices as a tool to monitor their eating habits for maintaining a healthy weight.

The **Canadian Diabetes Association** made changes to its meal planning system in 2004. Health Canada has also regulated the Nutrient Value labels found on most food products. Together with changes to medications and methods of managing diabetes, the association has developed the **Beyond the Basics** resource for meal planning. Beyond the Basics was created to help people eat healthy meals and thus follow a healthy lifestyle to promote good diabetes management, based on **Canada's Food Guide.**

The goal of Beyond the Basics is to assist people to include a variety of foods, based on **"Canada's Food Guide to Healthy Eating,"** and promote optimal diabetes management.

With information about carbohydrates people can keep their intake of carbohydrates consistent. A carbohydrate choice contains 15 grams of available carbohydrate (fiber is subtracted from total carbohydrate). Fruit, milk and starches are included in the carbohydrate choices. Vegetables are considered to be free when consumed in 1/2 cup (125 mL) portions. Visit **www.diabetes.ca** for information and resources from the Canadian Diabetes Association's website.

The **American Diabetes Association's Exchange Lists** have also been revised recently. They have developed the **Diabetes Food Pyramid,** grouping foods based on their carbohydrate and protein content in order to keep carbohydrate content consistent. This new list helps one get more variety through a flexible eating plan. Visit **www.diabetes.org** for the exchange list, the pyramid, information and resources from the American Diabetes Association's website.

Equipment List:	Per serving:	
BBQ or broiler pan	Calories	328
BBQ tongs	Fat	7.8 g
Large stove-top pot	Protein	26.5 g
Small stove-top pot	Carbohydrate	39.0 g
Cutting board	Fiber	4.9 g
Colander	Sodium	94 mg
Medium serving bowl		
Sharp veggie knife		
2 mixing spoons		
Fork		
Measuring cups and spoons		
Aluminum foil		

U.S. Food Exchanges:		Cdn. Food Choices:	
2	Starch	2 1/2 Carb	
3	Meat-lean	3	Meat/Alt
1	Vegetable		

Nutritional data, including food choices and exchanges, are calculated for the entire meal (per serving).

Sodium content is included for the benefit of those monitoring salt intake.

Canada's Choices and America's Exchanges are included for each meal in our book.

The Intimidated Weekday Cook

You may be a person who loves to cook or you may be the type who hates it. My observations have taught me that, whether you love it or hate it, chances are you really hate it in the workweek. Like any hobby or task we love to do, it turns into a chore when we are forced to do it. I can't tell you how many parents who love to cook tell me they are shocked that they fell into the "take-out trap." I have a saying which goes,

Take a look at the upcoming pages and take serious note of how these few things can change the task of weekday cooking, whether you like cooking or not.

Tools for Success

You decide to build a deck! (Yes, this is about food, I'm just odd!) You build partly for self-satisfaction and partly 'cause you don't have the money to pay to have it done…so you buy a book on how to build a deck. It tells you not to attempt the job unless you have a saw, a level, a hammer, a drill and a screwdriver. Of course, you will need to go off and purchase these essential tools. You can justify buying those tools because you know it will end up being a chore and cause nothing but frustration if you don't buy them to get the job done.

Yet, do you know how many families I have worked with that don't own a **sharp knife**? I most often hear, "I can't bear to spend that kind of money." A deck is a one-time project and you buy the tools. Dinner and good health are a lifelong project and you don't buy the tools? For some reason most people never make the connection that owning great tools makes cooking easier, especially for those who already find it a chore during the workweek!

Most people also don't know that it's a heck of a lot more dangerous to cut with a dull knife than a sharp one. Start your tool collection with a meat knife. It's an investment, so you want to stir up conversation with more than one person at a variety of kitchen shops. Feel the handle, find out about the metal used. Make your decision, and if you don't have the money, save a little each week until you do. Next, work toward owning a good veggie knife. What's the difference? **A meat knife is long and slender so that you can slice meat. A veggie knife is shorter and fatter so you can chop.**

Why do I push for every family to have two types of thermometers?

Indecision wrecks food. There is no self-satisfaction or reward for a dinner gone wrong. Owning these two little pieces of equipment removes the question, "I wonder if it's done yet?"

An **oven-safe thermometer** can be inserted into food as soon as you start cooking it. It's most commonly used to cook roasts or game. There is nothing like opening up the oven and knowing immediately how my meat is coming along! These types of thermometers also have a guide for safe cooking temperatures. Even when you aren't using it, you can still refer to it when cooking something else.

An **instant-read thermometer** is one you insert into the center of the food once it's cooked. It gives you an instant temperature read. This type is for testing things like the internal temperature of a chicken breast or hamburger. The oven-safe thermometer can usually be purchased at a grocery store. The instant-read will need to be purchased at a kitchen shop. Be prepared to pay $20-$30 for it. Once you own these and actually use them, your cooking, coincidentally, will have a much higher success rate.

A **slow cooker** is a great tool for one day each week and that one day can save the rest of your week. The reason I say this is because if you use it more than that, your family will get sick of having everything taste stewed, and you will end up putting it away and not using it at all. I recommend having two sizes. (You don't have one stove-top pot. One size doesn't fit all.) However, if you can only purchase one, get a medium-size capacity. It will do for most things.

A **salad spinner**, **two sets of measuring spoons** and a few **good cutting boards**. I use a salad spinner for more than salads. I rinse all sorts of veggies in the basket and safely spin them dry. I find it helpful for berries as well. I rinse all my herbs in the basket and spin them dry before I put them in the fridge. I recommend two sets of measuring spoons: one for wet ingredients and one for dry. If you have both out, the job gets done with ease. Buy a few good cutting boards so that you don't have to concern yourself with washing in between, one for meat, one for strong-smelling things like onion or certain spices and one for nonsmelly things. You won't always need all three, but when you do, it takes up no more room in the dishwasher than three plates and it's worth it to save you time.

BBQ grill pans. In many parts of the world, we think that grilling is only for the warm weather. I challenge people on this. Most climates don't get super cold or have heavy snowfall for more than 4 months per year MAX. That means there are 8 months left. If you have the right BBQ grill pans, you will find that a grill isn't just for grilling. They are so inexpensive to buy, but really expand the use of the grill to using it like an oven.

A **grilling cage or fish cage** is great to start with. I use this for veggie skewers, chicken wings (crunchy but not deep-fried), whole pieces of chicken, chops, fish, you name it. The beauty of it is that they are all in one basket, so you only have one thing to flip.

A **grilling wok** is essential for any stir-fry. It allows the stir-fry to have a smoky flavor.

A **BBQ grill pizza pan.** It's not only great for pizza, it works for fruit skewers, holding a roast for indirect heat cooking and a million other things, but I'm running out of room on this page.

We believe the last thing a person needs at the end of a long day is struggling to find their place on a recipe when making dinner.

We write our recipes from left to right in our trademark format,
written in the same way we read. Start at the top and follow from left to right to the end.

The symbols on the following page are used in this book
to make it even easier to get dinner on the table.

Look Before You Cook

Notice I never list weekly meals Monday through Friday. That's because I have no idea what your life is like each week. No one can tell you what type of meal you need on any given night except for you. You know who needs to go where, how much time you have or don't have and so on. Maybe you work Tuesday through Saturday.

Here is why you look at a recipe ahead of time. How many times have you started to prepare a meal only to find out the meat needed to be marinated for at least an hour? Get the picture? Along with our prep code we have visual triggers such as the crescent moon, a slow cooker or a BBQ. These will help you to decide if that meal coincides with your schedule the following night.

A **Crescent Moon** above the recipe alerts you to a 5- or 10-minute prep the night before so that the next day is ultra easy. Most of these can be started the same day, in the morning, if your schedule allows.

A **Slow Cooker** under the clock is a reminder you must prep the night before or the morning of your meal, using a slow cooker. The slow cooker fills you with wonderful feelings all day, knowing that when you get home, your dinner is ready or almost ready.

A **BBQ Grill** under the clock lets you know at least one portion of the meal is grilled. You may need to dig out a grilling pan if you don't own a BBQ grill. Grilling instructions are for a gas or propane grill. If you are using charcoals you will need to adjust.

The **Prep Code Clock** at the top right corner of each recipe tells you the "hands on" time it takes to prep dinner, after taking out the equipment and ingredients. This is why your first instruction in the recipe says: "Don't change yet. Take out equipment." I know that if you take out the equipment before you wind down in casual clothes, you have committed to making dinner...and you won't put the stuff back now, will ya?

We named this icon **Carrot Top** (I know I'm a little looped in the brain). He helps people who want to eat less meat or are vegetarian. You can find him on the About the Recipes pages with directions telling you what to do to make the meal meatless.

If you go to page 40 you will see Carrot Top on the left of some of the recipe descriptions. This icon indicates that there are instructions to convert that particular recipe to vegetarian. On page 41 you will see the names of the recipes, our family rating and a spot for your family rating. Kids love getting involved with rating a meal. Rate the meals from 1 to 10 and average your family's opinions. There are two pages just like these that precede each week. The advantage to having your family rate the meals is that it becomes an easy reference when creating a new meal plan and master shopping list.

A Shift in How You Do Things Can Make All the Difference

If you have teens, have them participate in cooking one meal per week. Most parents I meet feel sooo guilty about this. Why should you? You are giving your teens the most precious gift any parent could ever give, the gift of independence. They will be the university kids who aren't eating from a box (eventually). Buuuuuttt...give them the courtesy of asking which night would be best for them to do their part. I'm telling you, I have seen more budding teenage chefs over the years than I can count and just as many parents still trying to scrape their chins off the floor!

Don't even try to understand a teen's lunch...but I have the secret code after doing this with seven children. The lunch can't stink. It can't leave big things in your teeth. It can't make you look stupid while you eat (from their point of view, which is as mysterious as the pyramids). It can't be soggy and the container needs to be disposable! Knowing these mysterious teen truths, I suggest parents cut fruit and cheese and leave it out for them in the morning, 'cause that may be the only thing they eat until they get home. And health professionals, you may believe all your little solutions are going to change this. I guarantee you, as long as there is Stupid Teen TV, it won't, 'cause that's who they want to be like. You are boring and the TV people are cool...according to them!

The same rules apply for adults who don't cook. There is absolutely no excuse for this. I have been challenged by the toughest..."My husband hasn't cooked in thirty years; he's not going to start now." Oh, so your husband likes to be dependent on you? Try that one on them! Needless to say it always thrills me, but never shocks me when that same person reintroduces herself at a future conference or book signing saying, "Sandi, I can't get him out of the kitchen. In fact he asked me to pass on that you should try this one recipe of yours with mushrooms and a pinch of fines herbes! Ooooh, he's got it baaaad!"

Don't take hours on your weekend to cook for the week. Unless it's something you looove, you are going to burn out! But, **do prep little things**. If a recipe calls for half a bell pepper or onion, cut more and freeze them flat in a bag. (This way they defrost and break away from the bunch effortlessly.)

If you are making one meatloaf, make two and freeze the second. Remove the chicken tenders (fillets) from boneless, skinless chicken breasts and freeze separately. These come in awfully handy for quick chicken fingers or stir-fry. While slivering beef strips or cutting chicken into bite-size pieces, do extra and freeze them flat. If you coat chicken, fish or the like with a particular coating, use your blender or food processor to make a batch ahead. Keep it in the fridge for on-the-spot coating.

Before I get to answering some frequently asked questions on the next pages, I just want to say this. **When it comes to prepping ahead, doing little things makes a big difference.** Remember, cooking together is spending time together, so you really don't have to trade your health for time. The extra time you are looking for may be an extra set of hands, gaining independence, in the kitchen with you over a great cup of tea...and that's something they will always remember!

How-To's: Fish, Steak, Chicken

How do I cook fish?

Because of the natural shape of fish, thick to thin, some parts are going to cook faster than others if the thicker parts are not scored. Some people are really paranoid about not cooking fish to death and others like it more on the edge of juuust being cooked. If I am cooking a whole fish for company, everyone gets the doneness they like if I score the fish.

If the fish is really thick in the middle and really skinny at the ends, I tend to score my fish at the thicker parts. (Make little slits in the sides of the fish to even out the thickness throughout.) Or I tuck the skinny ends underneath to even it out a little. The heat needs to permeate the inside. This is why for quick cooking I almost always suggest using separate fillet pieces. It keeps things moving 'cause the heat can get to the inside from every direction. After lecturing you all on the necessities of an instant-read thermometer, you can test it out on your fish. The majority of people are most comfortable when the thickest part reaches 145° F, but you can go as low as 125°-135° F depending on the density of the fish. I like tuna rare. If you are not sure, you are better off to remove it from the heat a little early and let it rest.

Another way to check fish is to press on the fish with your finger. If the fish is done it will break into clean flakes. Because fish vary so much in size and density, it's not easy giving an exact equation, but these few tips will help you practice.

My favorite methods of cooking fish are:

In a cage on the BBQ grill
For this type of cooking you need to make sure the fish cage is well oiled before you put the fish in. I usually brown the outside and then use indirect heat to finish it up.

Searing the fish in a fry pan
I sear my fish on both sides, add the sauce I want to use, cover it up just before the fish is done and remove it from the heat. I let the steam from the liquid do the rest.

Oven cooking
This method is really easy and hands free. You can take the fish directly from oven to table. Preheat oven to 425° F. Grease your pan and place your spiced, plain or breaded fish in the pan for 15 minutes or until your instant-read registers at least 125°-145° F.

Plank cooking
The reason I love this method so much is because I can lay the whole fish fillet on the soaked cedar, toss on the spice, and the cedar, whether cooked in an oven or BBQ grill, gives the fish a unique flavor without adding calories. I like the BBQ grill better because it adds a smokier flavor, but it's pretty darned good in the oven too. For oven plank cooking follow the same instructions you would for grilling, but in a 400° F oven.

Paper bag cooking
I am famous for my paper bag cooking. I sear the fish in a pan with the spices I want and then I toss it in the oven on foil in a wet paper bag at 350° F for 15 minutes. I like this method for two reasons. It makes for a great presentation if you use individual lunch sacks (I serve them right on the plate), and it keeps even overcooked fish moister.

Why didn't my slow cooker recipe work?

Slow cookers have a common denominator with stove-top pots. That is, the recipe needs to match the size of pot. Here you see two pots with exactly the same capacity, yet if you cook the same stew in each, their consistency will be entirely different. The same goes for slow cookers. You need to watch carefully what capacity of slow cooker the recipe calls for. For example, when I make ribs I use a large-capacity slow cooker to boil them all day. When I am making something like stew or meat with a sauce, I tend to use a slow cooker with a smaller capacity, especially if I may be gone for longer than 8 hours, which most of us are.

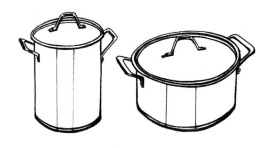

How do I light a BBQ grill? (For adults only!)

Don't laugh! Believe me when I tell you that most women I meet are petrified to light a gas BBQ grill. Now I get that, as a woman, I don't have the physical strength to do many jobs my husband can. But lighting a BBQ grill? Come on, ladies…here goes: **1.** Open the lid (this will ensure that you won't burn your hair off). **2.** Find where the gas or propane dial has an arrow indicating which way you need to turn the dial to open the gas valve. **3.** If you have an igniter, turn one side on while pressing the igniter until you see a flame. At that point, you can safely turn the other side on. The first side will ignite the other. If you do not have an igniter, you will need to purchase a long neck lighter. Most BBQ grills have a tiny hole on one side. Place the lit lighter in the hole (you need to crouch to do this) and turn the burner on closest to the hole. When the flame ignites, quickly remove the lighter and turn on the other side. Now you can open or close the BBQ grill for your cooking needs.

What kind of steak should I buy?

Everyone has a different answer to this question. I will tell you what works for me. For everyday eating I purchase a two-inch-thick cut of sirloin. If the supermarket doesn't have thick sirloin in a package, most supermarkets now have a meat counter. Ask the butcher to cut you a nice thick piece off a roast. When I am having company, or I want to make Ron or the kids a special steak dinner, nothing replaces tenderloin for me. I purchase the whole tenderloin and cut it into thick steaks myself. It's a lot more affordable that way. Notice I always say thick… for me this is key! If you have a thin steak, it's very difficult for the untrained cook to give each person a steak to the doneness which they prefer. However, if the steak is thick and you practice the "hand test" for steak doneness…in no time at all you will master a perfect steak and become known for your famous steaks!

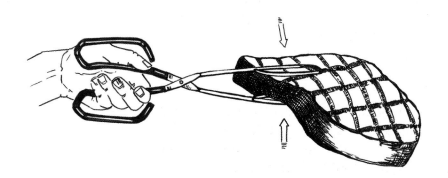

How do I cook a steak perfectly?

Step 1

Let the steaks sit out at room temperature for at least a 1/2 hour before cooking. Why? Think of a pound of cold butter. It's hard. The same pound of butter at room temperature is soft. Which one will you use to spread? If the oils in a steak have the chance to settle, the steak will cook more evenly. If the oils in the steak are able to rest *after* the steak is cooked, the oils once again redistribute themselves through the piece of meat. That may not be the most scientific way to describe it, but it's a description that makes sense to most people!

Step 2

Set your grill to medium heat (again, you have more control when the grill isn't set too high) and wait until it heats up. This takes about five minutes. Make your adjustments if using charcoal.

Step 3

Place your steaks on the grill. Give them a turn (not a flip) when they are easy to move and not before. Grill them for a few more minutes to ensure beautiful grill marks. Now you can flip and repeat the process on the other side.

Step 4

Take the steaks off the grill and wrap them in foil to rest *just* **before** the desired doneness. Meat continues to cook a little when resting.

Steak Doneness Hand Test

Touch the end of your pointer finger to the end of your thumb, without exerting any pressure. Then take the pointer finger of your other hand and poke the large part of your palm just at the base of the thumb. It will feel really mushy. That's what a rare steak feels like when you use your tongs to squish the center of the steak.

Now do the same thing, but bring a second finger against your thumb. Do you see how that same area has become firmer? That's what medium-rare steak feels like.

Now do the same thing, but bring a third finger against your thumb. Firmer again! That's what medium steak feels like.

All four fingers against your thumb will be the firmest, and that's what well-done steak feels like! YUCK! I…I mean wonderful for some of you!

How do I butterfly chicken?

We butterfly chicken either to create a slimmer wrapper to roll around other ingredients or to have the piece of chicken cook faster. The reason it's called "butterfly" is because you create a shape that looks somewhat like a butterfly.

The standard procedure is to hold the breast down with one hand and slice sideways through the breast to the tendon which joins the breast halves. As usual, I am going to break the rules of how to do this. Why? Most families, unfortunately, don't understand the importance of a good, sharp meat knife. Although I think they should own one, I know most don't, so unless you have a super sharp knife you will have trouble managing the standard procedure.

The first picture (illustration a) shows a single breast. Push the breast down sideways on the cutting board so that the breast is thick (illustration b). Slice down almost all the way through (illustration c). Push apart and flatten the sides to get similar results to the standard procedure.

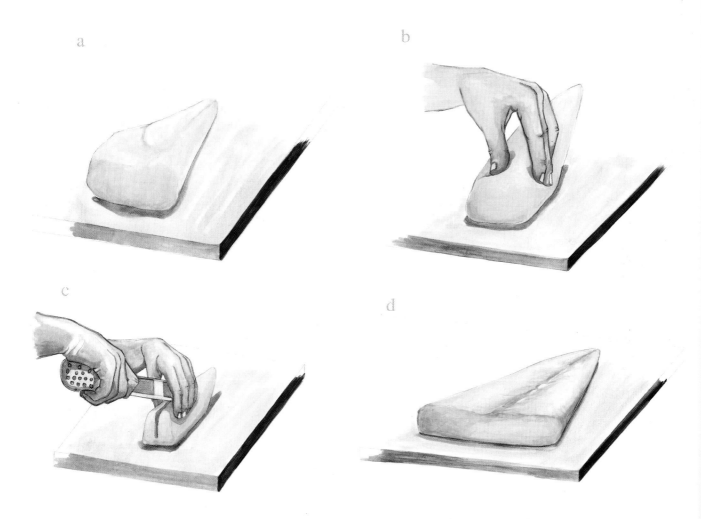

a   b   c   d

What about that little skinny piece of chicken on the back of the breast that sometimes looks like it may fall off?

Take that piece off first. It's called the fillet or chicken tender. You will see a little piece of white tendon on the top of it. Slice that little tough tendon off. I freeze these fillets flat in a freezer bag. They are great for quick chicken fingers or they defrost very quickly for a stir-fry or to cook and mix with a sauce.

Should I Microwave or Steam My Veggies?

I notice in this book you often steam the veggies? What's the difference?

Like everything else, we continue to learn about the science of food and how to cook it. I used to only microwave my veggies. A few years back I was a guest on Food Network in New York. I was very surprised when the host told me she didn't like microwaving anything. I started doing some research. I found the jury's still out on whether you should or shouldn't use a microwave. **There are good arguments for both sides.** One argument really made sense to me.

One side says that between 80-97% of the nutrients are depleted when using the stove-top method and that the nutrients are actually more intact if we use the microwave. The other side says that the **essential healing phytochemicals** (most of us hear the word antioxidants) found in vegetables are adversely affected by the microwave.

Sooooo, because my focus is meal planning, and I am not a scientist (I don't have a lab to measure phytochemicals) and because my goal is to help families get dinner on the table, and quickly, I did my own speed experiment. I took equal amounts of veggies; microwaved one batch and steamed the other. I put a small amount of water (about 1 cup) in the bottom of my stove-top pot and put the steamer basket with veggies on top with a lid. I turned the element to high heat. I then placed the same amount of veggies in a microwave-safe pot with lid and cooked them for the

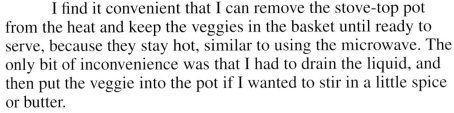

same amount of time (3-5 minutes depending on the veggie). **I was surprised when I realized that I enjoyed both the steamed and microwaved veggies the same.**

I find it convenient that I can remove the stove-top pot from the heat and keep the veggies in the basket until ready to serve, because they stay hot, similar to using the microwave. The only bit of inconvenience was that I had to drain the liquid, and then put the veggie into the pot if I wanted to stir in a little spice or butter.

We are tossed so much information that's it's really hard to know what is real and what is not. So sometimes I will steam my veggies and sometimes I will microwave them. You will make your own decision, keeping in mind that they both take the same amount of time.

Why? Why? Why?

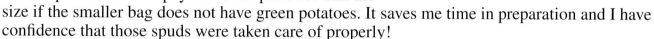

Why are parts of the potato green at times? Is it OK to eat the green part?

Stressful growing conditions and exposure to light can increase toxic alkaloids. In layman's terms, it's toxic stuff that helps make the potato the great tuber it is, but it's not so good if the levels get too high. Fortunately, the miracle of  God and nature has a built-in alert button for you in the color green. Because light induces chlorophyll formation (a clear indication the potato saw a lot more light than it should have), we know the toxic levels are too high. You must cut the green off. When I go grocery shopping, I take the time to look at my sack of potatoes. I will pay twice the price for half the size if the smaller bag does not have green potatoes. It saves me time in preparation and I have confidence that those spuds were taken care of properly!

What the heck is a rib of celery?

Plain and simple…it's one piece! The whole bunch is called a stalk. Some people say rib, some say stalk. It's confusing, so you need to use common sense. If the recipe asks for a stalk of celery, you need to evaluate whether celery is the main feature of the dish. If it's not, it likely means one piece.

Bell peppers can be so expensive. How do I pick a good one?

First you need to know that bell peppers are a fruit. The riper they get, the sweeter they get. That's why some people may hate green peppers and love red. The green peppers haven't ripened fully and therefore are not as sweet. In any case you only want to eat the outside, not the core  of seeds. Pick out a few with beautiful skin, then judge the weight of each with your hand. Sometimes you can get a huge pepper that's light and a small pepper that's heavy, depending on the seed core. Why buy a bunch of seeds if you don't use them! Purchase the one that weighs less.

Are the Food Guides Out of Date?

I believe, as I always have, that the Food Guides are right on track. The problem has been the people reading them!

Well…both the USDA Food Guide Pyramid and Canada's Food Guide can now be personalized to your needs by going to their websites.

Before, the guides didn't know how much exercise you got. They didn't know anything about you, so it was your responsibility to follow the guides according to your specific information. Now they do the thinking for you. You key in your information and they provide you with a plan customized to your needs. If you cut my plate into three parts, half would be veggies. The other half of the plate would be split between protein and grains. That's how the guide works for me. Why? Because I only manage to exercise three times a week, and the rest of the time I am standing at a kitchen counter or working at a computer. My daughter Paige, on the other hand, played college basketball and now coaches high school basketball while she's finishing her teacher's degree, so she needs a few more grains than I do because she is far more active.

We also have to look at the guide from a financial standpoint. When the kids were little I purchased far more things like pasta and bread because it was inexpensive and I had to make my dollar stretch. I was running from morning 'til night and as a sanity break had a brisk walk every morning, so I was able to burn off what I ate. You can't go heavy on bread and sweets if you're sitting at a computer all day, come home, then sit on the couch. You'll get fat! And if you have a really high metabolism, you may be skinny on the outside, but you're fat on the inside!

Go to mypyramid.gov or healthcanada. gc.ca/foodguide and enjoy their new interactive approach to making your eating life easier to understand.

CANADA
healthcanada.gc.ca/foodguide

The Prep Code

RED		YELLOW
	and	
Less Cutting and Chopping		More Cutting and Chopping

Dinner's ready in **30 minutes** or less
…when you need to get your butt out of the house fast.

GREEN		BLUE
	and	
Less Cutting and Chopping		More Cutting and Chopping

Dinner's ready in **60 minutes** or less
…when you have a small window of opportunity to prep,
but need to rush off somewhere while dinner is cooking,
or you want to relax before you eat.

The **symbols** on the left side of each recipe let you know what part of the meal you're
working on, at a glance! This also helps a person replace components if they want.
…you have leftover rice so you skip the starch.

● = protein component   ■ = starch component   ▲ = vegetable or fruit component

MEAL PLANS

About the Recipes

 Red

Over the years I have heard mixed reviews on chili. Some find it a family favorite and some have to deal with the yuuuuuck factor from their kids. I experimented to see if it was the flavor or texture that was the turn-off for some kids. Hands down, it was the various textures. So I kept the flavor, made it into a pasta sauce, served it with broccoli and *voilà*! A major hit with all the test families.
This is amazing with soy-based hamburger if you happen to be vegetarian.

 Green

This soup was inspired by a restaurant I was at. I thought, hmm, interesting, baked potato soup. I love the unique texture the potato skin adds to the soup. If I am in arm's reach of a BBQ I like to bake the potatoes at medium without the foil; this adds a smoky addition! Yum!

 Red

This recipe was a 10 out of 10 for almost every test family. One of our test families pointed out if you don't simmer the sauce on low when it says to, you lose out on the nummy sauce.
For vegetarians, fry up firm tofu until crisp, remove from pan, add sauce to pan, then put tofu back in the sauce.

Yellow

This is honestly one of the most delicious pork roasts you will ever eat. What I love about this meal is that it takes only a minute to prepare and then you come home to a house that smells like you have been cooking all day. Don't forget to get yourself an oven-safe meat thermometer if you don't have one. This is a prime example of how you don't have to think or worry about whether pork is fully cooked.

 Blue

One of our testers said had she seen this recipe in a book, she would have passed it by, but seeing she had to do it as her test commitment went ahead with it. She was shocked when her family gobbled it up!
If you are vegetarian, load this up with veggies and chickpeas and omit the chicken. It makes a great vegetarian stew-type meal.

Red: Not-So-Chili Pasta
with Broccoli (Bow Ties and Trees)

Our family rating: 10
Your family rating: _____

Green: Baked Potato & Cheddar Soup
with Dinner Rolls and Salad

Our family rating: 9.5
Your family rating: _____

Red: Ginger-Lime Chicken
with Rice, Zucchini and Mushrooms

Our family rating: 10
Your family rating: _____

Yellow: Oven Pork Roast with Applesauce,
Baby Potatoes, Gravy and Asparagus

Our family rating: 9.5
Your family rating: _____

Blue: Salsa-Cinnamon Chicken
with Couscous, Peas and Corn

Our family rating: 10
Your family rating: _____

Not-So-Chili Pasta with Broccoli
(Bow Ties and Trees)

Instructions:

Don't change yet! Take out equipment.
1. Fill a large **stove-top** pot with water. Cover and bring to a boil for pasta.

2. Heat oil in a large nonstick **fry pan** at medium-high. Finely chop onion, adding to pan as you slice. Cook, stirring occasionally, until caramelized. Add beef and spices to fry pan. Break up the beef with spoon. Brown until no longer pink.

   Add pasta sauce and broth to cooked meat and stir. **Reduce heat** to simmer.

3. Place pasta into boiling water and set timer according to package directions (approx 10 minutes).

4. Rinse broccoli in colander or steamer basket and cut into bite-size pieces (so they look like little trees). Place a small amount of water in the bottom of a **stove-top** pot with the broccoli in the basket above. *See page 34.*
   Let stand until timer rings for pasta.

   …when timer rings for pasta…
   Turn heat to high for broccoli. Reset timer for 3 minutes.

5. Rinse pasta under hot water in a colander. Add to meat pan, gently folding into sauce.

   When broccoli is tender but crunchy, dinner is ready to serve. Add a little butter if you must. We love grated Parmesan on the pasta. We also always put chili flakes on the table for those who like it hot!

Ingredients:

Take out ingredients.
water

1 tsp canola oil
1 medium yellow onion

1 lb or 450 g extra-lean ground beef
2 tsp chili powder
1 tsp ground cumin
pinch of turmeric

1 can pasta sauce (24 oz or 680 mL)
I like to use spicy.
1 cup beef broth, reduced-sodium

3 cups bow tie pasta

1 lb or 450 g broccoli florets

water

butter (optional)
Parmesan, grated, light (optional)

Serves 6

DINNER IS READY IN 25 MINUTES

Equipment List:

Large stove-top pot w/lid
Large nonstick fry pan
Cutting board
Colander
Stove-top pot w/steamer basket
Sharp veggie knife
Stirring spoon
Can opener
Measuring cups and spoons

Per serving:

Calories	450
Fat	12.6 g
Protein	25.7 g
Carbohydrate	58.4 g
Fiber	2.3 g
Sodium	711 mg

U.S. Food Exchanges:		Cdn. Food Choices:	
3	Starch	3	Carb
3	Meat-lean	3	Meat/Alt
1	Fat	1	Fat
1	Vegetable	1	Other Carb

15 to prep

Baked Potato & Cheddar Soup
with Dinner Rolls and Salad

Instructions:

Don't change yet! Take out equipment.
1. Preheat **oven** or BBQ grill to **400° F.**
   Wash potatoes and wrap in foil. Place in preheated oven. Set timer for 50 minutes.

2. Heat oil in a large **stove-top** pot at medium-high. Finely chop onion, adding to pot as you cut. Stir until onion is transparent and slightly brown.
   Add butter to onion pot and stir until melted. **Remove from heat.** Stir in flour. Gradually add broth and water, stirring constantly until smooth. Add spices and stir.

   Whisk in cream, milk and cheese. Let stand **off heat**.

   …when timer rings for potatoes…
   Let potatoes cool, then cut into bite-size chunks. Add to soup base. **Return soup to heat** on a low simmer, stirring occasionally.

3. Rinse lettuce in salad spinner and spin dry. Place in a large salad bowl. Chop any cold veggies you have on hand and add to bowl. Toss with dressing just before serving.
   I love a vinaigrette when my main dish is creamy, so I would pick balsamic, Italian or a sun-dried tomato dressing. My family also loves croutons on a tossed salad.

   When serving the soup, a few strands of chives and a sprinkle of cheddar really add a nice touch!

4. Serve with dinner rolls.

Ingredients:

Take out ingredients.

3 large potatoes (1 1/2 lbs or 1.35 kg)
aluminum foil

1 tsp canola oil
1/2 large sweet white onion

2 Tbsp butter
2 Tbsp flour
3 1/2 cups chicken broth, reduced-sodium
1 cup water
2 tsp garlic & herb seasoning, salt-free
1/2 tsp ground cumin
fresh pepper to taste
1/4 cup 10% cream
1/4 cup 1% milk
2 cups cheddar cheese, light, shredded

1 head green leaf lettuce
1 cup veggies (tomatoes, peppers, broccoli, carrots, etc.)
1/4 cup vinaigrette dressing, light (or your favorite)

croutons (optional)

chives, cheddar cheese (optional)

6 small whole-wheat dinner rolls

Serves 6

DINNER IS READY IN 60 MINUTES

Equipment List:

Large stove-top pot
Cutting board
Salad spinner
Large salad bowl
Salad tongs
Stirring spoon
Whisk
Soup ladle
Sharp veggie knife
Measuring cups and spoons
Aluminum foil

Per serving:

Calories	384
Fat	15.8 g
Protein	18.1 g
Carbohydrate	44.3 g
Fiber	6.2 g
Sodium	835 mg

U.S. Food Exchanges:	Cdn. Food Choices:
2 1/2 Starch	2 1/2 Carb
2 Meat	2 Meat/Alt
1 1/2 Fat	2 Fat

Ginger-Lime Chicken with Rice, Zucchini and Mushrooms

Instructions:

Don't change yet! Take out equipment.

1. Combine rice and water in a large microwave-safe pot with lid. **Microwave** at high 10 minutes, stir, then medium 10 minutes.

   …meanwhile…

2. Heat oil in a large nonstick **fry pan** or wok at medium-high.

   Cut chicken breast into bite-size pieces and add to pan as you cut. Stir until no longer pink. Add ginger, garlic and pepper. Stir.

   Add lime juice, brown sugar, sweet chili sauce and water to the pan. Stir and **reduce heat** to a low simmer.

   …while chicken is simmering…

3. Spray a large nonstick **fry pan** or wok with cooking spray and heat on medium. Wash and cut zucchini and mushrooms into large chunks, adding to pan as you cut. Spice and toss. Cook until tender but crisp.

4. When rice is ready, lift with a fork, cover and let stand for another 5 minutes.

   Serve the chicken and sauce directly on the rice or on the side. This is really simple, yet the flavor will knock your socks off!

Ingredients:

Take out ingredients.
1 1/2 cups basmati rice
3 cups water

1 Tbsp sesame oil

1 1/3 lbs or 600 g chicken breasts, boneless, skinless
1 1/2 Tbsp fresh ginger (from a jar)
   or 1 1/2 tsp ground ginger
1 Tbsp fresh garlic (from a jar)
   or 3 cloves minced
1/2 tsp black pepper

1/4 cup (overflowing) **lime juice**
3 Tbsp brown sugar
1-2 Tbsp sweet Thai chili sauce
   (depending on spice preference)
3/4 cup water

cooking spray
1 small zucchini
8 mushrooms
1 tsp garlic & herb seasoning, salt-free

Serves 4-6

DINNER IS READY IN 30 MINUTES

Equipment List:

2 large nonstick fry pans or
  woks
Large microwave-safe pot w/lid
2 cutting boards
Sharp meat knife
Sharp veggie knife
2 stirring spoons
Fork
Measuring cups and spoons

Per serving:

Calories	342
Fat	4.5 g
Protein	27.6 g
Carbohydrate	46.8 g
Fiber	1.8 g
Sodium	102 mg

U.S. Food Exchanges:		Cdn. Food Choices:	
3	Starch	3	Carb
2 1/2	Meat-very lean	2 1/2	Meat/Alt

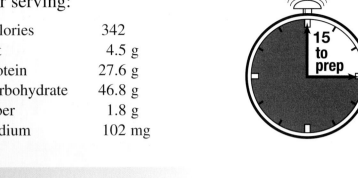

W
E
E
K

1

Oven Pork Roast with Applesauce, Baby Potatoes, Gravy and Asparagus

Instructions:

...the night before...
Take out equipment.

1. Place roast on a plate. Sprinkle with spices. Cover and let stand in **fridge** overnight.
   ...in the morning...
2. Preheat **oven** to **450° F.**
   Transfer roast to a shallow roasting pan. Place in preheated oven, uncovered. Set timer for 20 minutes. When timer rings **don't open the oven! Reduce heat** to **180° F.** That's it! Leave the roast in for up to 10 hours.

   ...when you get home...
3. Reset **oven** to **350° F.** Set timer for 30 minutes.

4. Wash potatoes and place in a large **stove-top** pot of cold water. Bring to a full boil, then **reduce heat** to a low boil until you can easily pierce the potato with a knife. Drain potato water into a large measuring cup and set aside. Add butter and spice to potatoes and swish to coat. Cover to keep warm.
   ...when timer rings for roast...
5. Transfer roast to plate. Wrap in foil to rest.

   Combine gravy mix and water in a cup, then whisk into roasting pan. Slowly whisk in potato water. Bring to a boil on high heat, stirring continuously. **Reduce heat** to simmer. Keep roast wrapped in foil, but drain juices from plate into roasting pan.

6. Snap off bottom nodes of asparagus and discard. Rinse in colander or steamer basket. Place a small amount of water in the bottom of a **stove-top** pot and bring to a full boil with the asparagus in the basket above. Cover and set timer for 4 minutes...or microwave for the same amount of time. *See page 34.*
   ...when timer rings for asparagus...
   Drain water. Toss in pot with butter and salt.

7. Combine applesauce and cinnamon in a small serving bowl to serve with pork roast.

Ingredients:

Take out ingredients.

3 lbs or 1350 g pork top loin roast, boneless, trimmed
1/2 tsp fresh ground pepper
1 tsp garlic powder
1 tsp Mrs. Dash Original seasoning

20 baby potatoes (or 4 large thin-skinned potatoes)

1 tsp butter
1/2 tsp dried rosemary leaves

aluminum foil
Gravy
3 Tbsp dry brown gravy mix *I like Bisto.*
3 Tbsp water
1 1/2 cups potato water *Add more if needed.*

20 asparagus spears

water

1 tsp butter (optional)
pinch of salt (optional)

1/2 cup applesauce, unsweetened
pinch of cinnamon
<u>Serves 4-6</u>   Assumes 1/3 roast left over.

DINNER IS READY IN 30 MINUTES

Equipment List:

...the night before...
Large plate
Measuring spoons
Plastic wrap
...in the morning...
Shallow roasting pan
...when you get home...
Large stove-top pot
Stove-top pot w/steamer basket
Large measuring cup
Small serving bowl
Large plate & Cup
Spatula & Whisk
Butter knife
Measuring cups and spoons
Aluminum foil

Per serving:

Calories	368
Fat	9.2 g
Protein	37.7 g
Carbohydrate	33.2 g
Fiber	4.9 g
Sodium	229 mg

U.S. Food Exchanges:		Cdn. Food Choices:	
2	Starch	2	Carb
4	Meat-lean	4	Meat/Alt

Assumes one-third roast left over.

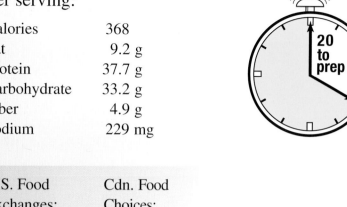

W E E K 1

Salsa-Cinnamon Chicken
with Couscous, Peas and Corn

Instructions:

Don't change yet! Take out equipment.

1. Heat a large nonstick **fry pan** at medium-high. Add pine nuts and toss until very light brown. Remove from pan and set aside.

   In the same, unwashed pan, heat oil at medium-high. Add chicken and brown on both sides. Add garlic to pan.

   ...while chicken is cooking...
   Combine salsa, water, craisins, honey and spices in a medium mixing bowl. Pour over browned chicken.
   Reduce heat to simmer. Set timer for 30 minutes.

   ...meanwhile...
2. Add water to a small **stove-top** pot and bring to a boil.
   Add onion flakes, bouillon, parsley and couscous to boiling water and stir. **Remove from heat.** Cover and let stand 5 minutes.

3. Rinse peas and corn together in a colander and place in a small microwave-safe pot with lid. **Microwave** at high for 3 minutes (or use a steamer basket in a stove-top pot). *See page 34.* Add butter if you must.

   If you have kids who don't like peas but love corn, add a few peas to the corn. Increase the amount you put in each time. Peas are loaded with fiber and iron, and corn and peas really complement each other.
   When I am just about ready to serve dinner, I like to add a little salsa and fresh cilantro to my couscous.

4. Sprinkle toasted pine nuts over chicken.
   It's sooo great!

Ingredients:

Take out ingredients.

1/2 cup pine nuts (can also use matchstick almonds)

1 tsp olive oil, extra-virgin
10-12 chicken thighs, boneless, skinless (1 1/2 lbs or 675 g)
1 Tbsp fresh garlic (from a jar)

1 3/4 cup chunky salsa
1/2 cup water
1/4 cup craisins (or raisins)
2 Tbsp liquid honey
1 1/2 tsp ground cumin
1 tsp cinnamon

3 cups water

2 tsp onion flakes
1 tsp vegetable bouillon powder
1 tsp dried parsley flakes
1 1/2 cups whole-wheat couscous

2 cups frozen baby peas
2 cups frozen corn

butter (optional)

2 Tbsp salsa (optional)
2 Tbsp fresh cilantro (optional)

reserved pine nuts

Serves 4-6

DINNER IS READY IN 40 MINUTES

Equipment List:

Large nonstick fry pan
Small stove-top pot w/lid
Small microwave-safe pot w/lid
Medium mixing bowl
Colander
Flipper
3 stirring spoons
Measuring cups and spoons

Per serving:

Calories	514
Fat	12.9 g
Protein	34.4 g
Carbohydrate	68.7 g
Fiber	11.5 g
Sodium	692 mg

U.S. Food Exchanges:		Cdn. Food Choices:	
3	Starch	3	Carb
3	Meat-lean	3	Meat/Alt
1	Fat	1	Fat
1	Vegetable	1	Other Carb

20
to
prep

About the Recipes

 Green

This recipe simply gives a regular hamburger a little pizzazz. If you are cooking for people who don't like spicy food, just make the burgers with everything except the horseradish and Tabasco, form a few burgers and then add those ingredients at the end for those who love spice.

Vegetarians, combine one-quarter cup mayo with the Tabasco, Worcestershire, chili powder and horseradish, then spread it on your bun. Grill up a veggie burger or portabella mushroom. It's really nice.

 Blue

These little puppies are addictive. They are easy to make and they are a great entertaining dish. I like to do the first four steps the night before. It only takes a few minutes and it makes the dinner even easier than it already is. If you like to entertain, I suggest you make double and freeze them individually on a sprayed cookie sheet. Once frozen, toss them in a freezer bag. Bake them fresh with the sauce, just before the guests arrive.

 Red

I love how tomatoes changed up this dish. Remember, it's really important to caramelize your onions first.

Replace the chicken with firm sautéed tofu and it's a great vegetarian dish. It's absolutely delicious either way.

 Yellow

I love creating recipes that have the flavor of a high-end restaurant, yet only takes minutes to make. It's a matter of using some of the same ingredients that a chef may use, like wine. You can use a nonalcoholic wine and the results are the same.

Vegetarians, grill a portabella and at the end melt some provolone cheese in the center. Drizzle with the sauce and scatter with pine nuts.

 Red

Families who tested this recipe thought it was worth finding the ingredients, as it was a number-one favorite with the kids. You can use regular mushrooms if you can't get the shitake or enoki. If you can't find miso paste you can replace it with a combination of 1 1/2 Tbsp of Marmite or Vegemite and 2 Tbsp of peanut butter, but it's not as good.

Vegetarians, leave out the chicken and add firm tofu.

Week 2

Green: Spiced Cheddar Burgers
with Cold Veggies and Dip

Our family rating: 9.5
Your family rating: _____

Blue: Spinach & Cheese–Stuffed Pasta Shells
with Caesar Salad

Our family rating: 9
Your family rating: _____

Red: Sweet & Sour Chicken
with Rice and Baby Carrots

Our family rating: 9
Your family rating: _____

Yellow: Steak with Red Wine Gravy, Crinkle Fries
and Roasted Parm Asparagus

Our family rating: 9.5
Your family rating: _____

Red: Udon Noodle Soup
with Crunchy Spinach Salad

Our family rating: 10
Your family rating: _____

Spiced Cheddar Burgers with Cold Veggies and Dip

Instructions:

Don't change yet! Take out equipment.
1. Preheat **BBQ grill** or grill pan to medium (**350° F**) by starting both burners on a medium-low setting.

   Mix together beef, Tabasco, Worcestershire, chili powder and horseradish in a bowl.
   Form the mixture into 8 large patties. Place on **BBQ grill** and close lid.
   Once hamburgers are easy to move, rotate each clockwise to create grill marks.
   Then flip and do the same on the other side.
   Do not overflip; this is why hamburgers fall apart. If the hamburgers flare up, use a squirt bottle of water to put out the flame.

   ...meanwhile...
2. Rinse baby carrots and snap peas. Rinse and cut broccoli into pieces. Rinse and slice zucchini and red pepper.

   Arrange veggies in a bowl alongside a smaller bowl of ranch dressing for dipping.

3. Check burgers with an instant-read thermometer and cook until the center is **170° F**. Top burgers with bacon and cheddar cheese. When burgers are almost done you can toast the buns on the upper rack of the grill. The cheese will melt while the buns are on the grill.

4. Slice tomatoes, then build your burger with your favorite toppings.

   It's fun to serve the burgers wrapped up in parchment with individual veggies and dip. But only if I have time!

Ingredients:

Take out ingredients.

2 lbs or 900 g lean ground beef
1 Tbsp Tabasco sauce
2 tsp Worcestershire sauce
1 tsp chili powder
1 Tbsp horseradish (optional)

squirt bottle of water (found at any home improvement store)

4 cups veggies (baby carrots, snap peas and broccoli)
1 small zucchini (or English cucumber)
1 red bell pepper
1/2 cup ranch dressing, fat-free

8 precooked bacon strips (optional)
1/2 cup cheddar cheese, light, shredded
8 multigrain hamburger buns

2 tomatoes
lettuce, mayonnaise, ketchup (optional)

Serves 4-6

DINNER IS READY IN 35 MINUTES

Equipment List:

BBQ grill (or grill pan)
Cutting board
Colander
Large mixing bowl
Large serving bowl
Small serving bowl
Hamburger flipper
Squirt bottle
Instant-read thermometer
Sharp veggie knife
Stirring spoon
Measuring cups and spoons
Parchment paper

Per serving:

Calories	583
Fat	20.8 g
Protein	42.0 g
Carbohydrate	57.8 g
Fiber	6.1 g
Sodium	860 mg

U.S. Food Exchanges:		Cdn. Food Choices:	
2 1/2	Starch	2 1/2	Carb
4 1/2	Meat-lean	5	Meat/Alt
2	Vegetable	1	Fat
		1	Other Carb

Prep Time

Spinach & Cheese–Stuffed Pasta Shells
with Caesar Salad

Instructions:

Don't change yet! Take out equipment.
1. Preheat **oven** to **375° F.**

2. Fill a large **stove-top** pot with water and bring
    to a boil for pasta.
    …meanwhile…
3. Drain spinach in a colander, using a fork to
    lightly squeeze out some of the water from the
    spinach.
    Combine spinach, egg and cheeses together in
    a medium-size mixing bowl.

    Finely chop or shred shallot and add to bowl.
    Add oil and stir. Cover and set aside in **fridge.**

4. Add pasta to boiling water and **reduce heat** to
    a medium boil.
    Set timer for 5 minutes. (You just want them
    softened, not completely cooked.)
    …when timer rings for pasta…
    Drain pasta in a colander, then rinse under
    cold water.
    Return to pot and gently toss with olive oil.

5. Stuff the spinach mixture into each shell with
    a small spoon and place, stuffed side up, in a
    large lasagna or cake pan.
    Cover with pasta sauce and place in preheated
    oven. Set timer for 30 minutes.
    …when timer rings for stuffed pasta…
    Remove pasta from **oven** and let stand while
    making salad.

6. Rinse lettuce in basket of salad spinner and
    spin dry. Place in large bowl and add bacon
    bits, croutons and Parmesan cheese if you
    wish. Toss with salad dressing right before
    dinner.

Ingredients:

Take out ingredients.

water

Spinach and Cheese Stuffing
3 1/2 oz or 100 g frozen chopped spinach,
  defrosted *You can run water over spinach in*
  a colander to defrost quickly.
1 egg
1/3 cup feta cheese, light, crumbled
1 cup ricotta cheese
1/2 cup cottage cheese, 1%
1/4 cup Parmesan cheese, light, grated
1/2 cup mozzarella cheese, part-skim,
  shredded
1 shallot
1 tsp olive oil, extra-virgin

24 large manicotti pasta shells
  (conchiglioni rigati), 8 oz or 225 g

1/2 tsp olive oil, extra-virgin

reserved spinach mixture
reserved pasta shells

1 can tomato-basil pasta sauce
  (24 oz or 680 mL) *I use the spicy variety.*

1 bag washed Romaine lettuce
  (12 oz or 350 g)
bacon bits, croutons and Parmesan cheese
  (optional)
1/3 cup Caesar salad dressing, light

Serves 4-6

DINNER IS READY IN 45 MINUTES

Equipment List:

Large lasagna or cake pan
Large stove-top pot
Cutting board
Colander
Medium mixing bowl
Salad spinner
Salad bowl
Salad tongs
Can opener
2 stirring spoons
Fork
Small spoon
Sharp veggie knife
Measuring cups and spoons

Per serving:

Calories	416
Fat	14.9 g
Protein	21.7 g
Carbohydrate	49.3 g
Fiber	3.1 g
Sodium	1025 mg

U.S. Food Exchanges:		Cdn. Food Choices:	
3	Starch	3	Carb
2	Meat-lean	2	Meat/Alt
2	Fat	2	Fat

20 to prep

WEEK 2

Sweet & Sour Chicken
with Rice and Baby Carrots

Instructions:

...the night before...
Take out equipment.

1. Combine sugar, pineapple juice, ginger, garlic, dry mustard, soy sauce, cider vinegar and tomatoes in a medium-size bowl. Cover and place in **fridge** overnight.

...when you get home...
2. Combine rice and water in a large microwave-safe pot. Cover and **microwave** at high 10 minutes, then medium 10 minutes.

...meanwhile...
3. Heat oil in a large nonstick **fry pan** at medium-high. Chop onion into quarters, adding to pan as you chop. Sauté until transluscent and caramelized. Cut chicken into bite-size pieces, adding to pan as you cut. Stir occasionally until no longer pink.
Slice celery and peppers into chunks, adding to pan as you cut.

Sprinkle with flour and stir.
Stir in sweet and sour sauce gradually, then add pineapple chunks. Stir and heat through.

4. When rice is ready, lift with a fork, cover and let stand for another 5 minutes.

5. Rinse baby carrots and serve with dinner, or as a snack while waiting for dinner to cook.

Ingredients:

Take out ingredients.
Sweet and Sour Sauce
1/3 cup dark brown sugar
pineapple juice, unsweetened (drained juice from a 14 oz or 398 mL can)
reserve pineapple chunks in fridge overnight
1/2 tsp ginger powder
1/2 tsp garlic powder
1/2 tsp dry mustard
1 Tbsp soy sauce, reduced-sodium
1/4 cup cider vinegar
1 can stewed tomatoes (14 oz or 398 mL)

1 1/2 cups basmati or white rice
3 cups water

1 tsp canola oil
1 medium onion

4 chicken breasts, boneless, skinless (1 1/2 lbs or 675 g)

1 rib celery
1/2 of a green bell pepper
1/2 of a red bell pepper

1 Tbsp flour
reserved sweet and sour sauce
reserved pineapple chunks

4 cups baby carrots (1 lb or 450 g)

Serves 4-6

DINNER IS READY IN 25 MINUTES

Equipment List:

...the night before...
Medium mixing bowl
Stirring spoon
Can opener
Measuring cups and spoons
...when you get home...
Large nonstick fry pan
Large microwave-safe pot w/lid
2 cutting boards
Colander
Sharp veggie knife
Sharp meat knife
Stirring spoon
Fork
Measuring cups and spoons

Per serving:

Calories	453
Fat	3.1 g
Protein	31.5 g
Carbohydrate	75.0 g
Fiber	4.9 g
Sodium	411 mg

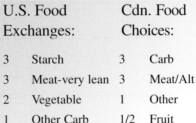

U.S. Food Exchanges:		Cdn. Food Choices:	
3	Starch	3	Carb
3	Meat-very lean	3	Meat/Alt
2	Vegetable	1	Other
1	Other Carb	1/2	Fruit

WEEK 2

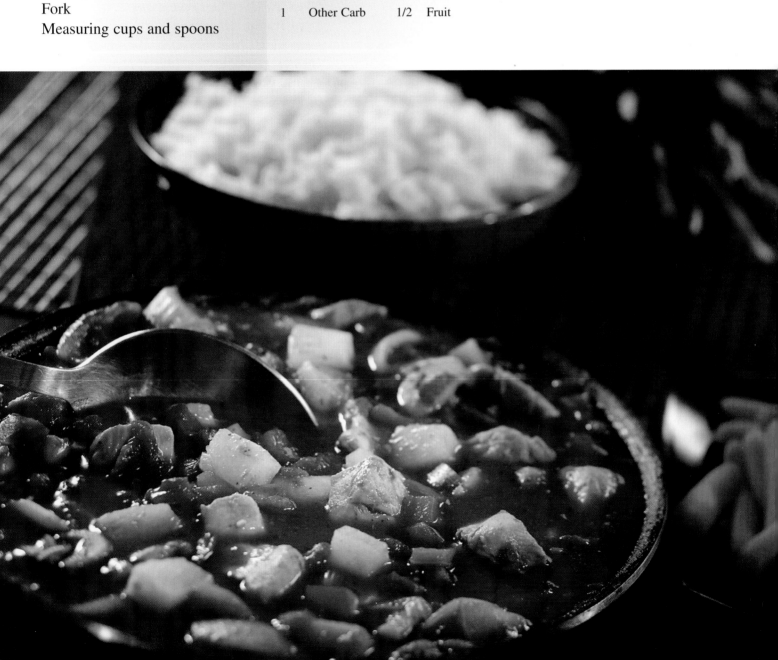

Steak with Red Wine Gravy, Crinkle Fries and Roasted Parm Asparagus

Instructions:

Don't change yet! Take out equipment.

1. **Remove steaks from refrigerator and let stand at room temperature.**
   Preheat **BBQ grill** or grill pan to medium. Preheat **oven** to **425° F.**

2. Melt butter and oil together in a medium **stove-top** pot at medium-high to start red wine gravy.
   Wash and finely chop green onions, adding to pan as you chop. Wash and slice mushrooms, adding to pan as you slice. Add garlic and spices to pan and stir. Stir in red wine and let mixture come to a boil. Gradually stir in mushroom soup, then whisk in milk.

   Place gravy mix in a small cup. Gradually blend in water, stirring constantly until smooth. Gradually stir into red wine gravy and **reduce heat** to a low bubbling simmer.

3. Place fries in a single layer on a cookie sheet. Sprinkle with seasoning salt if you wish. Place in preheated oven. Set timer for 10 minutes.
   …meanwhile…

4. Spray a large nonstick **fry pan** with cooking spray. Snap off bottom nodes of asparagus and discard. Rinse asparagus and add to pan. Sprinkle with grated Parmesan and let stand.

5. Place steaks on **BBQ grill** or grill pan. Rotate steaks clockwise, when they are easy to move, to create grill marks. Flip and repeat.
   Check out page 32 for the palm test to cook your steak just right. Keep practicing. You will become a pro!
   …when timer rings for fries…

6. Cook asparagus at medium, tossing occasionally, until tender but crunchy.

   When steaks are ready, let rest for a few minutes in foil. *To serve, pool gravy directly on serving plates, place steak on top, then drizzle a little gravy over one side.*

Ingredients:

Take out ingredients.

1 1/2 lbs or 675 g top sirloin or tenderloin steak, boneless, trimmed, 2 inches thick

Red Wine Gravy
1 tsp butter
1 tsp olive oil, extra-virgin

6 green onions
12 brown mushrooms
2 tsp fresh garlic (from a jar)
1 tsp Italian seasoning
1 tsp black pepper
1/4 cup red wine (can use nonalcoholic)
1 can cream of mushroom soup, reduced-sodium (10 oz or 284 mL)
1/2 the soup can of 1% milk

1 1/2 Tbsp dry brown gravy mix *I like Bisto.*
1 1/2 Tbsp water

1 lb or 450 g crinkle-cut French fries
seasoning salt (optional)

cooking spray, olive oil variety
1 lb or 450 g fresh asparagus

1/4 cup Parmesan cheese, light, grated

I do this entire meal on the BBQ grill, replacing the asparagus pan with a grill veggie wok. If you have a large enough BBQ grill with a side burner you can do the same.

aluminum foil

<u>Serves 4-6</u>

DINNER IS READY IN 30 MINUTES

Equipment List:

BBQ grill (or grill pan)
BBQ grill tongs
Cookie sheet w/sides
Large nonstick fry pan
Medium stove-top pot
Colander
Cutting board
Small cup
Corkscrew for wine
Whisk
Sharp veggie knife
Can opener
Stirring spoon
Measuring cups and spoons
Aluminum foil

Per serving:

Calories	407
Fat	14.3 g
Protein	33.7 g
Carbohydrate	36.9 g
Fiber	5.3 g
Sodium	459 mg

U.S. Food Exchanges:		Cdn. Food Choices:	
2	Starch	2	Carb
3 1/2	Meat-lean	3 1/2	Meat/Alt
1	Fat	1	Fat

W E E K 2

Udon Noodle Soup
with Crunchy Spinach Salad

Instructions:

Don't change yet! Take out equipment.
1. Rinse dry mushrooms in a colander, then place in a large mixing bowl.

Rinse udon noodles in the same, unwashed colander under cold water. Massage noodles gently with your fingers until they begin to separate…then add noodles to mushroom bowl.
Pour chicken broth all over noodles and mushrooms and let stand.

…meanwhile…

2. Heat oil in a large **stove-top** pot at medium-high. Cut chicken into bite-size pieces, adding to pot as you cut. Cook until no longer pink. Add ginger, garlic and miso paste to chicken. Stir.

Place the colander over the pot and drain the mushroom-noodle broth into the pot of chicken. Bring to a boil, then **reduce heat** to medium-low. Add the noodles and mushrooms. Slice green onions at an angle into 1/2" pieces. Set a few aside for garnish and add the rest to broth.

3. Rinse spinach in the basket of salad spinner and spin dry.
Place spinach on serving plates. Top with dry noodles and nuts. We also like to top with apple or mango slivers. Drizzle salad with dressing.

Garnish soup with the slivered green onion you set aside. YUUUMMMY, just like at a restaurant.

Ingredients:

Take out ingredients.
1/2 cup dry shitake mushrooms (or fresh enoki mushrooms)
People who don't like the texture or flavor of shitake or enoki mushrooms can use 1 1/2 cups regular mushrooms.

2 pkgs (7 oz or 200 g each) udon noodles (Japanese thick wheat noodles usually found fresh in your deli or dairy section) *You can replace with fresh Shanghai noodles.*

2 cartons chicken broth, reduced-sodium (30 oz or 900 mL each)

1 tsp canola oil
4 chicken breasts, boneless, skinless (1 1/3 lbs or 600 g)
1 tsp fresh ginger (from a jar)
1 tsp fresh garlic (from a jar)
1/4 cup miso paste (also called soybean paste, found with Asian foods) *Well worth finding because it lasts forever in the freezer.*

reserved noodles and mushrooms

4 green onions

1 bag washed baby spinach (8 oz or 225 g)

1 cup chow mein egg noodles
1/4 cup nuts (cashews, peanuts, almonds, pecans…your choice)
1 apple or mango (optional)
1/3 cup favorite light dressing
I like a ginger-wasabi dressing with this meal.

<u>Serves 4-6</u>
Assumes one-fourth soup left over.

DINNER IS READY IN 25 MINUTES

Equipment List:

Large stove-top pot
Large mixing bowl
2 cutting boards
Colander
Salad spinner
Salad tongs
Stirring spoon
Soup ladle
Sharp meat knife
Sharp veggie knife
Measuring cups and spoons

Per serving:

Calories	406
Fat	9.6 g
Protein	28.5 g
Carbohydrate	49.1 g
Fiber	2.9 g
Sodium	1207 mg

U.S. Food Exchanges:		Cdn. Food Choices:	
3	Starch	3	Carb
3	Meat-lean	3	Meat/Alt

Assumes one-fourth soup left over.

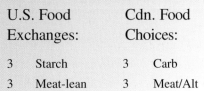

About the Recipes

Green

For those who love Peking duck there is no replacement; however, this is a fun replacement for everyday cooking. The secret to the authentic dish is to have really crispy skin. By removing the skin and then laying it back on top you can easily achieve this. You may prefer to have this with a side of broccoli and rice rather than using the cucumber and wraps. Either way it's a really fun dinner.

Blue

This recipe isn't fancy, but it's quick and it has that certain down-home something about it! If you like things a little spicier, add chili flakes, like we do.

If you are vegetarian, use soy-based hamburger instead of ground beef. Cook it a little longer, though, so the soy has a chance to absorb the flavors.

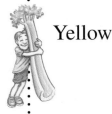

Red

These are a hit with kids. Remember to butter the bread sparingly before you slice the crusts off; it makes it waaaaay easier. These also freeze beautifully, so they are a great thing to make and freeze right after a turkey dinner. Bring these to a potluck and everyone will want the recipe.

If you are vegetarian you can load these with a blend of mushrooms, use a vegetable broth instead of consommé and use cornstarch to thicken. Remember to up your protein on the salad.

Yellow

If the pine nut and coconut turn out to be almost a crumbly paste, you got it right. This recipe is a hit, even with families who don't usually like fish. The melon really freshens up the flavor as well. Remember, cilantro is an acquired taste, so if you don't like cilantro…YET, leave it out and serve it on the side. If you are a vegetarian but don't eat fish, I can't help you with this one!

Yellow

I have always liked to boil ribs before BBQing. It gets rid of a bunch of fat and they are fall-off-the-bone tender. Boiling them used to deter me from having ribs during the workweek. By letting the slow cooker do this all day, ribs aren't just a weekend treat anymore! Teriyaki is a great replacement for strong garlic rib sauce.

Vegetarians can still enjoy the benefits of this meal by eating the grilled veggie salad with cashews and soy beans on top.

Week 3

Green: Sandi's Peking Chicken
                with Rice and Cucumber

> Our family rating: 9
> Your family rating: _____

Blue: Old-Fashioned Beef & Tomato Hash,
                Mashed Potatoes and Broccoli

> Our family rating: 8.5
> Your family rating: _____

Red: Chicken in Crunchy Bread Cups
                with Cranberries and Spinach Salad

> Our family rating: 10
> Your family rating: _____

Yellow: Pine Nut & Coconut–Crusted Salmon,
                Melon Salsa, Couscous and Asparagus

> Our family rating: 9
> Your family rating: _____

Yellow: Honey-Garlic Ribs
                with Grilled Veggie Salad

> Our family rating: 10
> Your family rating: _____

Sandi's Peking Chicken with Rice and Cucumber

Instructions:

Don't change yet! Take out equipment.

1. Preheat **oven** to **375° F.**
   Spray a broiler pan with cooking spray.
   Place chicken on broiler pan.
   Remove skin from each thigh. Transfer honey-garlic sauce to a small bowl, then brush onto the thigh and the back of the skin. Return the skin to the thigh and then generously brush the top of the skin. Repeat until all the thighs are done.

   Place chicken in preheated **oven**. Set timer for 40 minutes. Brush any remaining sauce on skin once or twice while cooking.

   Combine hoisin sauce, plum sauce and chicken broth in a small mixing bowl.
   Set aside.

   ...meanwhile...

2. Combine rice and water in a large microwave-safe pot with lid. **Microwave** at high 10 minutes, then medium 10 minutes.

3. Wash and cut cucumber into thin strips (approx 2 inches long).
   Cooked broccoli is another vegetable option that goes well with this meal.

4. When rice is ready, lift with a fork, cover and let stand for another 5 minutes.

   I like to make slits through the crunchy cooked skin before serving. Serve the chicken beside the rice with a side of cucumber. The sauce is to drizzle all over the chicken and rice.

   ...ooor we serve it this way...
   Soak rice papers in a bowl of lukewarm water. Place the bowl on the table and pull out one at a time. Slice the chicken into thin strips. Fill each wrap with chicken, rice and cucumber with a drizzle of sauce. YUM!!!

Ingredients:

Take out ingredients.

cooking spray
10 chicken thighs *with skin* **(2 lbs or 900 g)**
1 cup honey-garlic sauce *I like VH brand.*
  (or see page 74 to make your own honey-garlic sauce)

Sauce
1/2 cup hoisin sauce
1/4 cup plum sauce *I like VH brand.*
2 Tbsp chicken broth, reduced-sodium
  (or wine or water)

1 1/2 cups basmati or white rice
3 cups water

1 English cucumber

broccoli (optional)

Round rice papers (optional), found in ethnic section of supermarket

Serves 4-6

DINNER IS READY IN 45 MINUTES

Equipment List:

Broiler pan
Large microwave-safe pot w/lid
2 small mixing bowls
Cutting board
Basting brush
Stirring spoon
Sharp veggie knife
Sharp meat knife
Fork
Measuring cups and spoons

Per serving:

Calories	533
Fat	18.9 g
Protein	23.8 g
Carbohydrate	64.9 g
Fiber	1.9 g
Sodium	623 mg

U.S. Food Exchanges:		Cdn. Food Choices:	
4	Starch	4	Carb
2	Meat-med fat	2	Meat/Alt
2	Fat	2 1/2	Fat

Assumes half honey-garlic
sauce discarded.

15
to
prep

W
E
E
K

3

Old-Fashioned Beef & Tomato Hash, Mashed Potatoes and Broccoli

Instructions:

Don't change yet! Take out equipment.
1. Wash and peel potatoes.
   Cut potatoes into quarters and place in a large **stove-top** pot filled with cold water. Bring to a boil, then **reduce heat** to a low boil. Set timer for 10 minutes.

   ...meanwhile...
2. Brown ground beef in a large nonstick **fry pan** at medium-high.
   When meat is no longer pink, stir in tomatoes (with juice), corn, onion flakes and spices. **Reduce heat** to a simmer, stirring occasionally.

3. Rinse broccoli in a colander or steamer basket. Place a small amount of water in the bottom of a **stove-top** pot and bring to a full boil with the broccoli in the basket above. Cover and set timer for 3 minutes...or microwave for the same amount of time. *See page 34.* Add butter if you must.

   ...when timer rings for potatoes...
4. Drain potatoes and return to pot (no heat). Add butter, milk and spices. Whip until smooth with a hand masher or electric beaters.

   I like to smoosh my potatoes and meat together on my plate. My kids like it separate. Either way it's a simple, delicious, down-home meal.

Ingredients:

Take out ingredients.
4 large potatoes (2 lbs or 900 g)
water

1 1/2 lbs or 675 g ground beef, extra-lean

1 can Italian stewed tomatoes (19 oz or 540 mL)
1 cup frozen corn
I like the Peaches & Cream variety.
2 Tbsp onion flakes
1 tsp dried dill
1 tsp chipotle seasoning
1 tsp garlic & herb seasoning, salt-free

1 lb or 450 g broccoli florets
water

butter (optional)

1 Tbsp butter
1/4 cup 1% milk
1/2 tsp Mrs. Dash Table Blend seasoning
1/2 tsp dried parsley flakes

Serves 4-6

DINNER IS READY IN 35 MINUTES

Equipment List:

Large stove-top pot
Large nonstick fry pan
Stove-top pot w/steamer basket
Potato masher or electric
  beaters
Cutting board
Sharp veggie knife
Veggie peeler
Stirring spoon
Can opener
Measuring cups and spoons

Per serving:

Calories	370
Fat	8.6 g
Protein	31.8 g
Carbohydrate	44.1 g
Fiber	5.2 g
Sodium	327 mg

U.S. Food Exchanges:		Cdn. Food Choices:	
2	Starch	2	Carb
3 1/2	Meat-lean	3 1/2	Meat/Alt
1	Vegetable	1/2	Other Carb

W
E
E
K   3

Chicken in Crunchy Bread Cups
with Cranberries and Spinach Salad

Instructions:

Don't change yet! Take out equipment.
1. Preheat **oven** to **400° F.**

    Combine cornstarch, gravy mix, consommé and curry in a small **stove-top** pot at medium heat, stirring constantly until thickened. **Remove from heat** and set aside.

    Butter each slice of bread sparingly, then slice off crusts and discard.
    Press bread slices, butter side down, into muffin tins. Sprinkle poultry seasoning over each one.

    Finely dice chicken and add to a medium-size bowl as you cut. Finely chop green onions and mushrooms, adding to bowl as you cut. Stir to combine.
    Spoon chicken mixture evenly over bread in muffin cups. Drizzle consommé sauce on top of chicken mixture.
    Place in preheated **oven.**
    Bake for 8-10 minutes or until golden.

    ...meanwhile...

2. Rinse spinach leaves in a salad spinner and spin dry. Transfer spinach to individual serving plates. Sliver red pepper and sprinkle over spinach. Top with cashews if you wish. Drizzle with salad dressing.

3. Spoon cranberry sauce over hot chicken cups. Serve alongside salad.

    If you double this recipe, leftovers freeze beautifully and are great for entertaining. Rewarm in muffin tin until hot.

Ingredients:

Take out ingredients.

Consommé Sauce
1 Tbsp cornstarch
1 Tbsp dry brown gravy mix *I like Bisto.*
1 can consommé (10 oz or 284 mL)
1/2 tsp curry powder

2 1/4 tsp butter, softened (for all)
1 loaf bread, multigrain, sliced (18 slices)

1/2 tsp poultry seasoning (for all)

1 cooked deli roaster chicken (3 cups cooked diced chicken)
2 green onions
5 small mushrooms

1 bag spinach (12 oz or 350 g)

1/2 of a red bell pepper
1/4 cup cashews, unsalted (optional)
1/3 cup favorite salad dressing, fat-free

1/2 cup whole-berry cranberry sauce

Serves 4-6
Makes 18 chicken cups. Assumes 4 chicken cups left over.

DINNER IS READY IN 25 MINUTES

Equipment List:

Small stove-top pot
Small muffin tins
Medium-size mixing bowl
2 cutting boards
Salad spinner
Salad tongs
Sharp meat knife
Sharp veggie knife
Stirring spoon
Can opener
Butter knife
Spoon
Measuring cups and spoons
Individual serving plates

Per serving:

Calories	406
Fat	8.1 g
Protein	30.9 g
Carbohydrate	58.5 g
Fiber	13.3 g
Sodium	897 mg

U.S. Food Exchanges:		Cdn. Food Choices:	
3	Starch	3	Carb
3	Meat-lean	3	Meat/Alt

Assumes 4 chicken cups left over.

WEEK 3

Pine Nut & Coconut–Crusted Salmon, Melon Salsa, Couscous and Asparagus

Instructions:

Don't change yet! Take out equipment.
1. Preheat **oven** to **400° F.**
   Smash pine nuts and coconut together in a clean tea towel using a mallet or rolling pin until no chunks remain. *It almost seems like a paste until you move it around and break it up.* Set aside on a piece of waxed paper. Wash salmon under cold water.

   Place water in a shallow bowl and flour on a separate piece of waxed paper. Dip salmon fillets in water, then flour, then water again, then roll into nut mixture.
   This will create a glue-type coating.

   Spray a large nonstick **fry pan** with cooking spray. Sauté salmon over medium-high heat until nicely seared (approx 1 minute on each side or until each side is crispy). Transfer salmon onto a cookie sheet and place in preheated **oven.**
   Set timer for 7 minutes.
   …meanwhile…
2. Add water and broth to a small **stove-top** pot and bring to a boil.

   Add couscous to pot and stir.
   Remove from heat. Cover and let stand.

3. Snap off bottom nodes of asparagus and discard. Rinse in colander or steamer basket. Place a small amount of water in the bottom of a **stove-top** pot and bring to a full boil with the asparagus in the basket above. Cover and set timer for 4 minutes…or microwave for the same amount of time. *See page 34.*
   …when timer rings for asparagus…
   Drain water. Toss in pot with butter and salt.

4. Finely chop red onion and add to a small mixing bowl. Chop melon, tomatoes and cilantro and add to bowl as you cut.
   Serve beside cooked salmon.

Ingredients:

Take out ingredients.

1/2 cup pine nuts
1 Tbsp coconut, shredded, unsweetened

waxed paper
1 1/2 lbs or 675 g salmon fillets, boneless, skinless
1 cup water
1 cup flour
prepared nut mixture

cooking spray

3/4 cup water
1 can beef broth, reduced-sodium (10 oz or 284 mL)
1 cup couscous

20 asparagus spears

water

1 tsp butter (optional)
pinch of salt (optional)

Melon Salsa
1/8 of a red onion
1/4 of a cantaloupe
2 Roma tomatoes
1/4 cup cilantro

Serves 4-6

DINNER IS READY IN 25 MINUTES

Equipment List:

Large nonstick fry pan
Cookie sheet
Small stove-top pot w/lid
Stove-top pot w/steamer basket
Small mixing bowl
Shallow bowl
Cutting board
Sharp veggie knife
Flipper
Stirring spoon
Clean tea towel
Mallet or rolling pin
Can opener
Measuring cups and spoons
Waxed paper

Per serving:

Calories	414
Fat	11.4 g
Protein	31.9 g
Carbohydrate	45.4 g
Fiber	4.9 g
Sodium	210 mg

U.S. Food Exchanges:		Cdn. Food Choices:	
3	Starch	3	Carb
3	Meat-lean	3	Meat/Alt
1/2	Fat	1/2	Fat

20 to prep

Honey-Garlic Ribs
with Grilled Veggie Salad

Instructions:

…the night before…
Take out equipment.
1. Cut ribs into slabs and place them upright in crock of **slow cooker** as you cut. Sprinkle onion flakes over top.
Cover crock and place in **fridge** overnight.

…in the morning…
2. Return crock to the **slow cooker**. Add water to completely cover ribs. Cover with lid and set on low heat.

…when you get home…
3. Preheat **BBQ grill** or broiler to medium (approx **350° F**).
Drain ribs in colander.
Spray ribs with cooking spray. Place on **BBQ grill** or broiler pan. Sear each side.
Brush ribs with honey-garlic sauce.
Reduce heat to medium-low (**300° F**). Turn ribs often, brushing with remaining sauce.

4. Slice peppers, zucchini, onion and mushrooms in large chunks and place in **BBQ grill wok** or stove-top wok as you cut. Dab with pesto.

Place on **BBQ grill** or stove-top at medium. Set timer for 15 minutes, tossing a few times. *You will need to check.*

…meanwhile…
5. Rinse lettuce in basket of salad spinner and spin dry. Drizzle with salad dressing.

…when timer rings for veggies…
Remove ribs from **BBQ grill** or broiler and veggies from BBQ grill or stove-top.

Top salad with grilled veggies.
Serve with bread rolls if you like.

Ingredients:

Take out ingredients.
2 1/2 lbs or 1125 g lean pork ribs, back or side (can double the amount to have extras)
3 Tbsp onion flakes

water

cooking spray

1 jar honey-garlic sauce (12 oz or 341 mL)
I like VH brand.
(or make your own honey-garlic sauce by combining 1/4 cup sugar, 1/4 cup honey, 1/2 cup soy sauce, 1 Tbsp molasses, 4 cloves minced garlic, 1/2 cup water)

1 red bell pepper
1 green bell pepper
1 small zucchini
1 onion
10 mushrooms
1 Tbsp basil pesto

1/2 bag Romaine lettuce (6 oz or 175 g)
1/4 cup favorite salad dressing, fat-free

6 bread rolls (optional)

Serves 4-6

DINNER IS READY IN 30 MINUTES

Equipment List:

...the night before...
Slow cooker
Cutting board
Sharp meat knife

...when you get home...
BBQ grill (or broiler)
BBQ grill wok or stove-top wok
BBQ tongs
Colander
Cutting board
Salad spinner & Salad tongs
Flipper
Basting brush
Sharp veggie knife
Individual serving plates
Measuring cups and spoons

Per serving:

Calories	477
Fat	28.8 g
Protein	24.7 g
Carbohydrate	29.5 g
Fiber	2.3 g
Sodium	391 mg

U.S. Food Exchanges:		Cdn. Food Choices:	
1 1/2	Starch	2	Carb
3	Meat-high fat	3	Meat/Alt
1	Fat	4	Fat
1	Vegetable		

Assumes half honey-garlic
sauce discarded.

About the Recipes

Red

Over and over again parents were shocked by their family's reaction to this recipe. If you don't eat shrimp, make everything the same but sauté bite-size pieces of chicken first. The flavor of this dish is addictive, so I suggest you serve your plates and get the rest in the fridge quickly, or portion control may be out of the question!

If you are vegetarian, sauté firm tofu strips until well browned, remove and continue with sauce, adding strips later.

Green

Our readers find the chicken thigh meals to be some of their favorites and this is no exception. Some people want to make this with chicken breast, and that's fine. Just keep in mind, though, that if you are eating a lot of chicken the thigh has more iron, so I suggest you change it up.

Red

Many families were shocked by how their kids gobbled up the hog-town pizza from our first book, *Life's on Fire*. We have been combining strange ingredients on pizza for years, and now it's something our readers are counting on…and Don and Nik, you only won the pizza contest because of the biased voting from your nieces and nephews! Rematch? Remember, you can also use a premade crust for this pizza, but I have to say for this particular one, I like the refrigerated-in-a-tube kind or a homemade thin pizza crust.

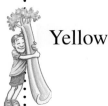

Yellow

I personally love this recipe with lamb, but if you just don't care for lamb, it's great with pork chops, chicken or beef. The combined flavors enhance any meat. Dried apricots can usually be purchased in the bulk bins, so you don't have to worry about storing leftover packages; however, if you do have to buy a pack, they store for ages and are a delicious and nutritious snack alone!

The combined flavors also enhance the flavor of any vegetable if you want to make this vegetarian. Add chickpeas for protein.

Blue

I warn you, this salad is addictive. When it comes to the burgers, many families wondered why I combined turkey and chicken. I find the combination makes them less dry. If you think your kids won't like the hot pepper jelly on their bun, you can use apple jelly instead.

Vegetarians, you can toss this salad with chickpeas and/or tofu. It will take on the flavor of the dressing, and I tell you it's a meal on its own with a nice chunk of focaccia, yuuummmy!

Week 4

Red: Creamy Pesto Shrimp (or Chicken)
with Linguini and Asparagus

> Our family rating: 10
> Your family rating: _____

Green: Sweet Soy Chicken
with Rice and Broccoli

> Our family rating: 10
> Your family rating: _____

Red: Apple Feta Pizza
with Spinach Salad

> Our family rating: 9.5
> Your family rating: _____

Yellow: Lamb (or Pork) Masala
with Rice and Peas

> Our family rating: 9
> Your family rating: _____

Blue: Cordon Bleu Burgers
with Cranberry Cabbage Salad

> Our family rating: 8.5
> Your family rating: _____

Creamy Pesto Shrimp (or Chicken) with Linguini and Asparagus

Instructions:

Don't change yet! Take out equipment.

1. Fill a large **stove-top** pot with water and bring to a boil.

2. Heat butter and olive oil in a large nonstick **fry pan** at medium-low.
   Remove from heat and whisk in flour. Slowly whisk in milk until smooth. Return to medium-low heat. Season with pepper. Heat through while whisking. **Reduce heat** to simmer white sauce.

3. Place pasta in boiling water.
   Set timer for 10 minutes.

   …meanwhile…
4. Whisk cheese into white sauce until well combined. Blend in pesto.
   If the sauce gets too thick it's OK to keep adding a little bit of milk at a time.
   Fold shrimp into sauce and heat through.

5. Snap off bottom nodes of asparagus and discard. Rinse in colander or steamer basket. Place a small amount of water in the bottom of a **stove-top** pot and bring to a full boil with the asparagus in the basket above. Cover and set timer for 4 minutes…or microwave for the same amount of time. *See page 34.*
   …when timer rings for asparagus…
   Drain water. Toss in pot with butter and salt.

   …when timer rings for pasta…
6. Rinse pasta in colander and return to pot, no heat.

   Serve shrimp and sauce over linguini.
   I like hot chili flakes sprinkled on mine.

Ingredients:

Take out ingredients.
water

White Sauce
1 Tbsp butter
1 Tbsp olive oil, extra-virgin
2 Tbsp flour
2 cups 1% milk
1/2 tsp pepper

12 oz or 375 g linguini pasta

2/3 cup Parmesan cheese, grated, light
1/4 cup basil pesto

1 lb or 450 g large shrimp, cooked, peeled and deveined

20 asparagus spears (1 lb or 450 g)

water

1 tsp butter (optional)
pinch of salt (optional)

hot chili flakes (optional)

Serves 4-6

DINNER IS READY IN 25 MINUTES

Equipment List:

Large stove-top pot
Large nonstick fry pan
Stove-top pot w/steamer basket
Colander
Whisk
Stirring spoon
Measuring cups and spoons

Per serving:

Calories	431
Fat	13.5 g
Protein	31.3 g
Carbohydrate	45.8 g
Fiber	2.5 g
Sodium	487 mg

U.S. Food Exchanges:		Cdn. Food Choices:	
2	Starch	3	Carb
3	Meat-lean	3	Meat/Alt
1	Fat	1	Fat
1	Milk-low fat		

Sweet Soy Chicken with Rice and Broccoli

Instructions:

Don't change yet! Take out equipment.
1. Preheat **oven** to **350° F**.

2. Combine rice and water in a large oven-safe casserole with lid. Cover and place in preheated **oven**. Set timer for 60 minutes.

   …meanwhile…
3. Unravel chicken thighs and place in a large lasagna or cake pan. *You may need to squish them together to fit.*
   Combine brown sugar, vinegar, soy sauce, water, ginger and garlic in a small mixing bowl. Drizzle evenly over chicken.
   Place chicken in **oven** next to rice (chicken actually cooks for 40-45 minutes).

   …when timer rings for rice and chicken…
   Turn oven off.

4. Rinse broccoli in colander or steamer basket. Place a small amount of water in the bottom of a **stove-top** pot and bring to a full boil with the broccoli in the basket above. Cover and set timer for 3 minutes…or microwave at high for 3 minutes. *See page 34.*
   Add butter if you must.

   I love the sauce from the chicken drizzled over the rice.

Ingredients:

Take out ingredients.

1 1/2 cups basmati rice
3 cups water

10-12 chicken thighs, boneless, skinless
  (1 3/4 lbs or 800 g)

1/2 cup brown sugar
1/4 cup vinegar
1/4 cup soy sauce, reduced-sodium
1/4 cup water
1 Tbsp fresh ginger (from a jar)
1 Tbsp fresh garlic (from a jar)

1 lb or 450 g broccoli florets
water

1 tsp butter (optional)

Serves 4-6

DINNER IS READY IN 60 MINUTES

Equipment List:

Large oven-safe casserole w/lid
Large lasagna or cake pan
Stove-top pot w/steamer basket
Small mixing bowl
2 stirring spoons
Measuring cups and spoons

Per serving:

Calories	417
Fat	5.9 g
Protein	31.8 g
Carbohydrate	58.8 g
Fiber	1.1 g
Sodium	495 mg

U.S. Food Exchanges:		Cdn. Food Choices:	
3	Starch	3	Carb
3	Meat-very lean	3	Meat/Alt
1	Other Carb	1	Other Carb

Apple Feta Pizza with Spinach Salad

Instructions:

Don't change yet! Take out equipment.
1. Preheat **oven** to **375° F.**

2. Heat oil in a large nonstick **fry pan** at medium-low. Sliver onion, adding to pan as you cut. Stir occasionally until limp and caramelized (for this pizza we need 'em sweet). Set aside.

   Slice apple into thin wedges and set aside.
   Slice eggplant into thin slices and set aside.

3. Unroll pizza dough and place on a small cookie sheet with sides. Press dough with the palms of your hands to cover pan. Brush top of crust with oil using a pastry brush and sprinkle evenly with spices.

   Layer with caramelized onion, feta cheese, Parmesan cheese, eggplant, apple, asparagus and mozzarella cheese.

   Place in preheated **oven** for 25 minutes or until crust is golden brown.

   ...meanwhile...
4. Rinse spinach in basket of salad spinner and spin dry. Place spinach on individual serving dishes. Sliver red onion. Sprinkle onion, feta cheese, mandarin oranges and cashews over spinach.

   Drizzle with salad dressing. *My family loves Vidalia onion or poppy seed on this salad.*

Ingredients:

Take out ingredients.

1 tsp olive oil, extra-virgin
1 large onion

1 Macintosh or Spartan apple
1 cup sliced eggplant or zucchini

1 Pillsbury pizza crust, in a tube
  (10 oz or 284 g)
1 tsp olive oil, extra-virgin
1 tsp Italian seasoning
chili flakes (optional)

caramelized onion
1/4 cup feta cheese, light, crumbled
2 Tbsp Parmesan cheese, light, grated
reserved eggplant or zucchini slices
reserved apple slices
6 asparagus spears
1/2 cup mozzarella cheese, part-skim,
  shredded

1 bag baby spinach (12 oz or 350 g)

1/8 of a red onion
1/4 cup feta cheese, light, crumbled
3 mandarin oranges, segmented (or 1 can
  mandarin oranges, drained)
1/2 cup cashews, unsalted
1/3 cup favorite salad dressing, fat-free

<u>**Serves 4**</u>

DINNER IS READY IN 30 MINUTES

Equipment List:

Large nonstick fry pan
Small cookie sheet with sides
Cutting board
Salad spinner
Sharp veggie knife
Pastry brush
Stirring spoon
Individual serving dishes
Salad tongs
Measuring cups and spoons

Per serving:

Calories	496
Fat	18.8 g
Protein	19.8 g
Carbohydrate	69.3 g
Fiber	7.4 g
Sodium	1083 mg

U.S. Food Exchanges:		Cdn. Food Choices:	
3	Starch	3	Carb
2 1/2	Meat	2 1/2	Meat/Alt
2	Fat	2	Fat
1	Fruit	1	Fruit

15 to prep

Lamb (or Pork) Masala with Rice and Peas

Instructions:

...the night before...
Take out equipment.

1. Melt butter in a large nonstick **fry pan** at high. Place lamb chops in pan and brown on both sides. Sprinkle chops with onion flakes.

...meanwhile...
Place diced tomatoes with juice, broth, wine and peanut butter in center crock of **slow cooker**. Add spices and stir to combine.

Add lamb chops to center crock and scrape the onions and remaining butter into the crock with a spatula.

Score apricots and add. Add cinnamon and stir. Cover and place in **fridge**.

...in the morning...

2. Return center crock to slow cooker and place on low heat.

...when you get home...

3. Combine rice, water and cloves in a large microwave-safe pot with lid. **Microwave** at high for 10 minutes, then medium for 10 minutes. *You don't eat the cloves...they are only added for the aroma and taste.*

4. Rinse peas in colander or steamer basket. Place a small amount of water in the bottom of a **stove-top** pot and bring to a full boil with the peas in the basket above. Cover and set timer for 2-3 minutes. Or **microwave** on high for 3-4 minutes, then let stand. *See page 34.*

*Serve with naan bread if you wish. I preheat the **oven** to **350° F**, toss the naan in, then turn the oven off. Store it in a covered dish to keep it warm at the table. OK! I can't stand it...my mouth is having a fit and I want this RIGHT now!*

Ingredients:

Take out ingredients.

1 Tbsp butter
2 lbs or 900 g lamb chops, bone-in, trimmed *You can use pork, but lamb is my family's favorite.*
1/4 cup onion flakes

1 can diced tomatoes (14 oz or 398 mL)
1 can beef broth, reduced-sodium (10 oz or 284 mL)
1/2 cup white wine or water
2 heaping Tbsp peanut butter, light
1/4 tsp ginger powder
1 Tbsp garam masala (spice blend)
1/2 tsp curry powder

2-3 dried apricots (can buy these in bulk section of store)
1/2 of a cinnamon stick

If you need to cook this for more than 6 hours, add an additional cup of water. *Read about slow cookers on page 31.*

1 1/2 cups basmati rice
3 cups water
4-5 whole cloves (optional)

4 cups frozen peas
water

4-6 pieces naan bread (optional)

<u>**Serves 4-6**</u>

DINNER IS READY IN 25 MINUTES

Equipment List:

…the night before…
Slow cooker
Large nonstick fry pan
Cutting board
Sharp veggie knife
Stirring spoon
Flipper
Spatula
Can opener
Measuring cups and spoons
…when you get home…
Large microwave-safe pot w/lid
Stove-top pot w/steamer basket
Serving dish w/lid for naan
Measuring cups and spoons

Per serving:

Calories	598
Fat	23.1 g
Protein	38.5 g
Carbohydrate	58.6 g
Fiber	7.2 g
Sodium	446 mg

U.S. Food Exchanges:		Cdn. Food Choices:	
3	Starch	2 1/2	Carb
4	Meat-med fat	4	Meat/Alt
1/2	Fat	2	Fat
1	Vegetable	1	Other Carb

20 to prep

Cordon Bleu Burgers
with Cranberry Cabbage Salad

Instructions:

Don't change yet! Take out equipment.

1. Finely chop green onion and add to a large salad bowl as you chop. Add coleslaw mix, nuts, steam-fried noodles, craisins, sugar, spices, rice vinegar, canola oil and sesame oil. Stir until well combined. Set aside in **fridge**.

2. Preheat **BBQ grill** or grill pan to medium-low. Combine chicken, turkey, egg, cornflake crumbs and spices in a medium-size bowl, then form into 6 burgers.

   Spray both sides of burgers with cooking spray and place on preheated **BBQ grill**. Rotate burgers clockwise to create angled grill marks when they can be easily lifted from grill. Flip burgers and repeat. Once almost cooked, top with Swiss cheese and ham.
   *Use an instant-read thermometer to ensure the burgers are fully cooked to **180° F**.*

3. Spread one side of bun with mayo and other side with hot pepper jelly.

   Everyone can add their own favorite toppings.

Ingredients:

Take out ingredients.
2 green onions (white and green parts)
4 cups coleslaw mix (8 oz or 225 g)
2 Tbsp pecan pieces (or 1 Tbsp pecans and 1 Tbsp matchstick almonds)
1 cup steam-fried egg noodles
1/4 cup craisins
1 1/2 tsp sugar
1/4 tsp pepper
pinch of salt
1/2 tsp garlic & herb seasoning blend, salt-free
1 Tbsp rice vinegar
1 Tbsp canola oil
1/2 tsp sesame oil

3/4 lb or 350 g lean ground chicken
3/4 lb or 350 g lean ground turkey
1 egg
1/2 cup cornflake crumbs
1/2 tsp smoked paprika
   (or 1/2 tsp paprika + 1/4 tsp Liquid Smoke)
1/2 tsp onion powder
1 tsp mustard powder
1 tsp grill spice blend, salt-free

cooking spray

2 oz or 57 g Swiss cheese, light, thin slices
2 oz or 57 g shaved honey or Cajun ham, lean, cooked

6 hamburger buns, multigrain
1 1/2 Tbsp mayonnaise, light (optional)
2-3 Tbsp hot pepper jelly, either red pepper or jalapeño (optional, but amazing)

Optional Toppings
tomato, lettuce, onion

Serves 4-6

DINNER IS READY IN 40 MINUTES

Equipment List:

BBQ grill (or grill pan)
Cutting board
Sharp veggie knife
Large salad bowl
Salad tongs
Stirring spoon
Medium-size mixing bowl
Flipper
Instant-read thermometer
Butter knife or spreader
Measuring cups and spoons

Per serving:

Calories	595
Fat	23.6 g
Protein	43.1 g
Carbohydrate	54.6 g
Fiber	5.3 g
Sodium	716 mg

U.S. Food Exchanges:		Cdn. Food Choices:	
3	Starch	3	Carb
5	Meat-med fat	5	Meat/Alt
1	Vegetable	2	Fat
		1/2	Other Carb

About the Recipes

Green

The only complaint families had on this one was that they wanted more chicken because they loved it so much. Well, portion control is all up to you guys. I can't help you with that! This really is a great meal, though. If you like a little more sauce, just add a little more water than what's called for.

Blue

A lot of people like quiche, but not a lot of people want to bother with crust, especially not during the workweek. This is a great way to get the best of both worlds. What I also love about quiche is that you can make it anything you want, similar to pizza. I used to add pizza sauce to quiche when the kids were little. I would put some pepperoni in and call it pizza quiche.
With or without meat, this dish served with salad is one of my favorites.

Red

With a little prep the night before, it's amazing how beautiful a steak dinner can be. Stuffed potatoes are also easy to freeze, so if you are going to the trouble I suggest you make extra and tuck them away for a night gone wild! You can have a regular Caesar salad with this meal, but I love throwing it on the grill to get that smoky flavor…and it looks incredible.
Vegetarians, load up the potatoes with nuts, salsa and cheese with the delicious Caesar on the side.

Yellow

This recipe is great, but you have to make sure you don't use a pot that has a super-wide surface, or the chicken will end up dry. If you are a sauce fan, you can remove the chicken when the sauce is almost done and add a little flour and milk. Then put the breasts back in for a bit. Either way, this meal is packed with flavor.

Red

The reason I say bok choy or broccoli is because you can't always get bok choy. So we tested it with both, and either way it's fantastic.
If you are vegetarian and don't eat seafood, you can soak either tofu or cooked canned lentils or chickpeas in the dressing, then toss all that into the bok choy to heat through.

Week 5

Green: Sassy Chicken Thighs
with Pasta and Broccoli

> Our family rating: 10
> Your family rating: _____

Blue: Crustless Quiche
with Spinach Salad

> Our family rating: 9.5
> Your family rating: _____

Red: BBQ Steak and Stuffed Potatoes
with Grilled Caesar Salad

> Our family rating: 10
> Your family rating: _____

Yellow: Feta & Broccoli–Stuffed Chicken,
Rice and Bean Medley

> Our family rating: 8
> Your family rating: _____

Red: Thai Citrus Shrimp on Bok Choy
(or Broccoli) with Egg Noodles

> Our family rating: 8.5
> Your family rating: _____

Sassy Chicken Thighs with Pasta and Broccoli

Instructions:

Don't change yet! Take out equipment.
1. Preheat **oven** to **350° F**.

   Unravel chicken thighs and place in a large lasagna or cake pan. *You may need to squish them together.*
   Combine water, ketchup, sweet chili sauce, fish sauce, garlic and spices in a small mixing bowl. Pour evenly over chicken. Bake in preheated **oven** uncovered. Set timer for 35 minutes.
   (Note: Actual baking time for chicken will be about 50 minutes.)

   ...meanwhile...
2. Rinse broccoli and place in colander or steamer basket. Place a small amount of water in the bottom of a **stove-top** pot. Cover and let stand (no heat) until timer rings.

   ...when timer rings for chicken...
   (Leave chicken in. This is simply a reminder to start the pasta.)

3. Fill a large **stove-top** pot with water. Cover and bring to a boil.
   Once water has come to a full boil, toss pasta in and set timer according to package directions (approx 10 minutes).

   ...meanwhile...
4. Bring broccoli water to a boil and once it's boiling, **reduce heat** to low. This will steam the broccoli slowly while pasta is cooking.

   ...when timer rings for pasta...
5. Drain and rinse the pasta in a colander, then return to pasta pot. Toss with a little olive oil if you like. *We also enjoy tossing on a little dried basil. Enjoy!*

Ingredients:

Take out ingredients.

10-12 chicken thighs, boneless, skinless (1 3/4 lbs or 800 g)

1/4 cup water
1/4 cup ketchup
1/2 cup sweet Thai chili sauce
2 Tbsp fish sauce
1 1/2 tsp fresh garlic (from a jar)
2 tsp paprika
1/4 tsp Chinese five spice powder
1/4 tsp lemon pepper

1 lb or 450 g broccoli florets
water

water

4 cups cavatappi pasta (10 oz or 283 g)
You can use any spiral pasta.

1 tsp olive oil, extra-virgin (optional)
1/2 tsp basil leaves (optional)

Serves 4-6

DINNER IS READY IN 60 MINUTES

Equipment List:

Large lasagna or cake pan
Stove-top pot w/steamer basket
Large stove-top pot w/lid
Small mixing bowl
2 stirring spoons
Colander
Measuring cups and spoons

Per serving:

Calories	415
Fat	6.3 g
Protein	35.0 g
Carbohydrate	53.1 g
Fiber	2.2 g
Sodium	944 mg

W
E
E
K

5

U.S. Food Exchanges:		Cdn. Food Choices:	
2	Starch	2 1/2	Carb
4	Meat-lean	4	Meat/Alt
1	Vegetable	1	Other Carb
1	Other Carb		

Crustless Quiche with Spinach Salad

Instructions:

Don't change yet! Take out equipment.

1. Preheat **oven** to **375° F**.
   Add butter and oil to a large nonstick **fry pan** over medium heat. Finely chop onion and add to pan as you chop. Sauté until just translucent. **Remove from heat.**

   Whisk egg whites until frothy in a medium mixing bowl. Add yolks, cream, milk, biscuit mix and pepper. Whisk together until well blended. Scrape butter and onion from fry pan into egg mixture using a spatula.
   Stir until well combined.
   Spray a 9-inch pie plate (glass is best) with cooking spray. Pour egg mixture into pie plate.

   Chop broccoli into small bite-size pieces and sprinkle over egg mixture in pie plate. Slice and add mushrooms, then shrimp, or whatever else you like. *I love zucchini and tomato. The sky's the limit...as long as it fits in the pan!*

   Grate cheeses and sprinkle over egg mixture. Bake in preheated **oven** on lower rack for 45 minutes or until top is golden brown and inserted knife comes out clean.

   ...while quiche is cooking...

2. Sprinkle matchstick almonds and pecan pieces onto a large cake pan. Drizzle with honey and sprinkle with a tiny bit of salt. Place in **oven** on top rack for about 5 minutes...*Don't leave their sight; when you smell them, they are ready to take out.* Let nuts cool but keep scraping and tossing them until they don't stick to the pan anymore.

3. Rinse spinach in basket of salad spinner, spin dry and place on dinner plates. Sliver pepper and red onion. Layer these over the spinach, sprinkle with blueberries and nuts, then drizzle with your favorite dressing.

Ingredients:

Take out ingredients.

1 tsp butter
1 Tbsp olive oil, extra-virgin
1/3 cup onion (1/4 of an onion)

4 large eggs (separated)
1/4 cup 10% cream
3/4 cup 1% milk
1/2 cup biscuit mix *I like Bisquick.*
1/4 tsp fresh ground pepper

cooking spray

1/2 cup broccoli florets (or any other green veggie you have on hand)
4 mushrooms
1 cup shrimp, cooked, deveined (optional)
1/2 cup zucchini (optional)
1 Roma tomato (optional)

1/4 cup Gruyère cheese
1/4 cup mozzarella cheese, part-skim
1/2 cup cheddar cheese, light

Yummy Salad Nuts
1 cup matchstick almonds
1 cup pecan pieces
1 tsp liquid honey
pinch of salt
You will only use 2 Tbsp for the meal. You might as well make up a jar for the next time. We even sprinkle them on cereal and yogurt!

1 bag baby spinach (12 oz or 350 g)
1/4 of a red bell pepper
1/8 of a red onion
1 cup frozen wild blueberries
1/4 cup fruit vinaigrette, light (or your favorite dressing)

Serves 4

DINNER IS READY IN 55 MINUTES

Equipment List:

Large nonstick fry pan
9" pie plate (glass is best)
Large cake pan
Medium mixing bowl
Salad spinner
Salad tongs
Individual serving plates
Cutting board
Sharp veggie knife
Whisk
Cheese grater
Flipper
Butter knife
Stirring spoon
Spatula
Measuring cups and spoons

Per serving:

Calories	403
Fat	23.6 g
Protein	20.4 g
Carbohydrate	28.3 g
Fiber	4.3 g
Sodium	576 mg

U.S. Food Exchanges:		Cdn. Food Choices:	
1	Starch	1	Carb
2 1/2	Meat-mod fat	2 1/2	Meat/Alt
2	Fat	3	Fat
2	Vegetable	1/2	Other Carb

20 to prep

WEEK 5

BBQ Steak and Stuffed Potatoes
with Grilled Caesar Salad

Instructions:

…the night before…
Take out equipment.
1. Preheat **oven** or BBQ grill to **425° F.**
   Scrub the outside of potatoes and place in
   oven on rack or on BBQ grill, unwrapped.
   Set timer for 45 minutes.
   …when timer rings…
   Remove potatoes from oven, and when they
   are cool enough to be handled, cut them in
   half lengthwise. Scoop the insides of potato
   into a bowl, leaving the skin intact.
   Mash butter, sour cream, garlic, milk, spices
   and potatoes together until smooth. Spoon
   potato mixture back into skins. Sprinkle with
   cheese. Cover and place in **fridge**.

   …just before dinner…
2. Preheat **BBQ grill** or grill pan to medium
   (**350° F**).
   Place stuffed potatoes in small cake pan, then
   on top rack of **BBQ grill** or in 300° F oven.
   Heat through until the rest of dinner is ready.
   Prepare optional toppings for stuffed potatoes
   and set aside on table.
   …meanwhile…
3. Slice complete head of lettuce into quarters
   lengthwise, keeping the core intact. Rinse each
   wedge gently under tap and pat dry. Brush cut
   sides with olive oil and place on **BBQ grill** cut
   side down. When edges begin to char and curl,
   transfer to individual serving plates.

4. **Grill** steaks, rotating clockwise to create grill
   marks. Flip, then brush steaks with BBQ
   sauce. Slightly undercook steaks to your
   preference, as they keep cooking while resting
   in foil. *See the hand test on page 32.*

5. Combine dressing, mayonnaise and milk
   in a bowl, stirring until smooth. Drizzle
   wedges with dressing, then top with croutons,
   Parmesan cheese and bacon bits if you like.

Ingredients:

Take out ingredients.

2 large baker potatoes (1 lb or 225 g)
*Stuffed potatoes freeze beautifully, so if you
can, make extra.*

1 tsp butter
1/4 cup sour cream, no-fat
1/2 tsp fresh garlic (from a jar)
1/4 cup 1% milk
pinch salt and pepper to taste
1/2 tsp parsley flakes
1/2 cup aged cheddar cheese, light, shredded

prepared stuffed potatoes

Optional Potato Toppings
**green onion or chives, cheese, bacon bits
and sour cream**

1 large head Romaine lettuce
2 tsp olive oil, extra-virgin

*This Caesar salad has a great presentation
and an amazing smoky flavor!*

**1 1/2 lbs or 675 g top sirloin steaks or
tenderloin, 2 inches thick, boneless, trimmed**
1/2 cup BBQ sauce, your favorite
aluminum foil

Lower-Fat Gourmet Caesar Dressing
**3 Tbsp gourmet Caesar salad dressing,
  lower-fat**
3 Tbsp mayonnaise, no-fat
2 Tbsp 1% milk
1/2 cup croutons
1 Tbsp Parmesan cheese, light, grated
1/4 cup bacon bits (optional)
Serves 4-6

DINNER IS READY IN 25 MINUTES

Equipment List:

...the night before...
Cutting board
Small mixing bowl
Potato masher
Sharp veggie knife & Spoon
Measuring cups and spoons
...just before dinner...
BBQ grill (or grill pan)
Small cake pan
Cutting board
2 small mixing bowls
2 basting brushes
Sharp veggie knife & Flipper
Individual serving plates
Measuring cups and spoons
Aluminum foil

Per serving:

Calories	346
Fat	12.4 g
Protein	32.9 g
Carbohydrate	25.7 g
Fiber	4.5 g
Sodium	562 mg

U.S. Food Exchanges:	Cdn. Food Choices:
1 1/2 Starch	1 1/2 Carb
4 Meat-lean	4 Meat/Alt

W
E
E
K

5

Feta & Broccoli–Stuffed Chicken, Rice and Bean Medley

Instructions:

Don't change yet! Take out equipment.

1. Crumble feta into a small mixing bowl. Finely chop broccoli and green onion, adding to bowl as you cut. Add spice, stir and set aside.

Butterfly each chicken breast by slicing down the center of the thickest portion, BUT NOT ALL THE WAY THROUGH, the entire length of the breast. Open the split breast and this will make a large thin piece of chicken.

Smear garlic on cut side of each chicken breast, then spoon equal amounts of the broccoli mixture in the center of each piece. Roll the breast around the stuffing and secure with a toothpick.

Heat oil in a small to medium-size nonstick **fry pan** at medium-high. **The size of pan is very important or the chicken will be dry.** Brown chicken on all sides. Once browned, add wine and chicken broth to pan. Cook uncovered, turning once. If liquid is evaporating, **turn heat down**. When chicken is cooked through, cover and **remove from heat**. (Instant-read thermometer will read **180° F.**) *If liquid evaporates before chicken is done, add a bit more wine, broth or water.*

…while chicken is simmering…

2. Combine rice and water in a large microwave-safe pot or casserole dish with lid. **Microwave** at high 10 minutes, then medium 10 minutes.

…meanwhile…

3. Heat olive oil in a different large nonstick **fry pan** at medium-high. Rinse bean medley in a colander and add to pan. Add lemon pepper and soy sauce. Toss to coat, then **reduce heat** to medium-low. Stir often, until beans are hot and tender but still a bit crunchy.

Ingredients:

Take out ingredients.

1/4 cup feta cheese, light
  (can replace with shredded cheddar)
1 cup broccoli florets
1 green onion
1/2 tsp Mrs. Dash Original seasoning

**4 chicken breasts, boneless, skinless
(1 1/2 lbs or 675 g)**
See page 33 for illustrations on how to butterfly a chicken breast.

1 tsp fresh garlic (from a jar) for each breast
reserved broccoli mixture
toothpicks

1 tsp olive oil, extra-virgin

1/2 cup dry white wine (can be nonalcoholic)
**1 can chicken broth, reduced-sodium
(10 oz or 284 mL)**

1 1/2 cups basmati or white rice
3 cups water

1 tsp olive oil or butter
4 cups frozen mixed bean-carrot medley
  (if not available use green beans)
1/2 tsp lemon pepper
2 tsp soy sauce, reduced-sodium

<u>**Serves 4-6**</u>

DINNER IS READY IN 30 MINUTES

Equipment List:

Small to medium nonstick fry
pan w/lid
Large nonstick fry pan w/lid
Large microwave-safe pot w/lid
2 cutting boards
Sharp veggie knife
Sharp meat knife
Small mixing bowl
Corkscrew for wine
Colander
Flipper
Instant-read thermometer
2 stirring spoons
Can opener & Spoon
Measuring cups and spoons
Toothpicks

Per serving:

Calories	366
Fat	5.5 g
Protein	34.5 g
Carbohydrate	43.8 g
Fiber	3.6 g
Sodium	367 mg

U.S. Food Exchanges:		Cdn. Food Choices:
2	Starch	2 1/2 Carb
3 1/2	Meat-very lean	3 1/2 Meat/Alt
2	Vegetable	

20 to prep

WEEK 5

Thai Citrus Shrimp on Bok Choy (or Broccoli) with Egg Noodles

Instructions:

Don't change yet! Take out equipment.

1. Fill a large **stove-top** pot with water and bring to a boil for rice noodles.

2. Rinse bok choy (or broccoli) in a colander and set aside.

3. Soften peanut butter in a small bowl for 5-10 seconds in the **microwave**.
   Whisk the following ingredients into the softened peanut butter to make the dressing: brown sugar, mandarin orange juice, lime juice, fish sauce, ginger and sweet chili sauce. Finely mince lemongrass and add. Set aside.

4. Add noodles to boiling water. Set timer for 8 minutes or follow package directions.

   …meanwhile…

5. Heat oil in a large nonstick **fry pan** or wok at medium. Toss in bok choy (or broccoli). Add 1/3 of dressing to pan, toss and cover. Let steam for a couple minutes.
   Add shrimp. Keep tossing to heat through and wilt bok choy (or until broccoli is tender but crunchy).

   …when timer rings for noodles…

6. Rinse noodles in colander. Mound noodles in the center of each dinner plate. Top with bok choy (or broccoli) and shrimp, then drizzle with remaining dressing. Top with reserved mandarin orange segments.

   Our family likes to sprinkle cashews and fresh cilantro on top. You can also serve fresh mandarin oranges and grape tomatoes on the side…but only if you have time!

Ingredients:

Take out ingredients.
water

1/2 lb or 225 g bok choy (or broccoli, 1-2 heads)
Dressing
2 Tbsp peanut butter, light
1 Tbsp brown sugar
juice from mandarin orange container (single-serve size, 3 1/2 oz or 107 mL, approx 1/3 cup) *Set oranges aside.*
1 Tbsp lime juice
1/4 cup fish sauce
2 tsp fresh ginger (from a jar)
1 tsp sweet Thai chili sauce (optional)
1 Tbsp lemongrass (you can replace fresh with lemongrass in a tube or grated lemon rind)

10 oz or 284 g rice noodles

2 tsp sesame oil
reserved bok choy (or broccoli)
1/3 prepared dressing

1 lb or 450 g large shrimp, cooked, deveined with tails

reserved mandarin oranges from container

cashews (optional)
fresh cilantro (optional)
2 fresh mandarin oranges (optional)
8-12 grape tomatoes (optional)

Serves 4-6

DINNER IS READY IN 30 MINUTES

Equipment List:

Large stove-top pot
Large nonstick fry pan w/lid
  or wok
Colander
Small bowl
Whisk
Stirring spoons
Individual serving plates
Measuring cups and spoons

Per serving:

Calories	314
Fat	4.5 g
Protein	19.1 g
Carbohydrate	48.2 g
Fiber	1.6 g
Sodium	1227 mg

U.S. Food Exchanges:		Cdn. Food Choices:	
2	Starch	2	Carb
2	Meat-lean	2	Meat/Alt
1	Other Carb	1	Other Carb

15 to prep

About the Recipes

Red

All I can say is that I love this meal and so does anyone who makes it! If you are vegetarian you can pan fry some firm tofu, remove and then load up on extra veggies…but, man I love the flank steak in this recipe…juuuust my personal opinion!

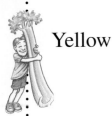

Yellow

I developed this recipe for a wonderful couple on one of my shows. The wife loved tomatoes and the husband hated them, but for some strange reason he liked bruschetta. By having a family pizza made this way, Dad didn't pass on his dislike for tomatoes to his little one, and Mom got to enjoy one of her favorite ingredients.

Green

If you follow the steak doneness hand test on page 32, you get the same results without the grill marks. Remember to take the steaks off the heat prior to your preferred doneness. They will finish cooking while resting. If you don't drink brandy (we don't) you can buy one of those tiny bottles, or just use apricot or apple jelly.

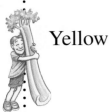

Yellow

One of my best friends, Kathy, introduced me to gumbo. She gave me a recipe and warned me that I may not love her as much as soon as I saw the ingredients. Kathy claimed, while introducing me as a keynote speaker at a conference, that my response was, "Don't worry, I'll fix it." Now…although I don't remember ever saying that, I have to say, I was shocked that my health nut friend digested that much fat and salt in one sitting. Needless to say I had to do a little fixing!

Vegetarians who don't eat seafood, replace the shrimp and sausage with a can of mixed beans (chickpeas, black eyed peas…).

Blue

The original test families that we brought so many meals to for so many years are going to be jumping for joy when they see this recipe. Every time we create a new book, I forget to include it!

Vegetarians, load up the center with eggplant or other veggies of choice and use a vegetable broth to make the cubes.

Week 6

Red: Hoisin Slivered Beef
                  with Green Beans and Basmati Rice

> Our family rating: 10
> Your family rating: _____

Yellow: Bruschetta Pizza
                  with Spinach Salad

> Our family rating: 9
> Your family rating: _____

Green: Steak with Peppercorn Brandy Sauce,
                  Corn on the Cob and Mixed Greens

> Our family rating: 9.5
> Your family rating: _____

Yellow: Quick Louisiana Gumbo
                  with Rice and Broccoli

> Our family rating: 9
> Your family rating: _____

Blue: Chicken en Croute
                  with Strawberry Skewers

> Our family rating: 9.5
> Your family rating: _____

Hoisin Slivered Beef with Green Beans and Basmati Rice

Instructions:

Don't change yet! Take out equipment.
1. Combine rice and water in a large microwave-safe pot with lid. **Microwave** at high for 10 minutes, then medium 10 minutes.

2. Heat oil in a large nonstick **fry pan** or wok at medium-high. Cut beef into thin short strips, against the grain, adding to pan as you cut. Toss and sauté slightly. Add garlic and ginger to pan.

   Reduce heat to medium-low.
   Add soy sauce, rice vinegar, fish sauce, sweet chili sauce, hoisin sauce and chili paste. Stir to combine.

   ...when timer rings for rice...
3. Lift rice with a fork and let rest for 5 minutes.

4. Rinse beans in a colander under cold water. Add to meat pan and stir. When beans are hot and tender, but still crunchy, they are ready.

   This is juuust one of those meals we could have over and over again!

Ingredients:

Take out ingredients.
1 1/2 cups basmati rice
3 cups water

1 tsp olive oil, extra-virgin
1 1/2 lbs or 675 g flank steak, trimmed

2 tsp fresh garlic (from a jar)
1 Tbsp fresh ginger (from a jar)

1/4 cup soy sauce, reduced-sodium
1 Tbsp rice vinegar
2 Tbsp fish sauce
2 Tbsp sweet Thai chili sauce
2 Tbsp hoisin sauce
1/2 tsp Sambal Oelek (crushed chili paste)
  (optional)

1 lb or 450 g frozen green beans

Serves 4-6

DINNER IS READY IN 30 MINUTES

Equipment List:

Large microwave-safe pot w/lid
Large nonstick fry pan or wok
Cutting board
Colander
Sharp meat knife
Stirring spoon
Fork
Measuring cups and spoons

Per serving:

Calories	385
Fat	7.8 g
Protein	30.0 g
Carbohydrate	48.4 g
Fiber	3.6 g
Sodium	1027 mg

15
to
prep

U.S. Food Exchanges:		Cdn. Food Choices:	
3	Starch	3	Carb
3	Meat-lean	3	Meat/Alt

W
E
E
K

6

Bruschetta Pizza
with Spinach Salad

Instructions:

Don't change yet! Take out equipment.
1. Preheat **oven** to **375° F**.

2. Cut tomatoes into small chunks, adding to a large mixing bowl as you cut.
   Finely chop green onion, adding to bowl as you chop. Crush garlic and add to bowl.

   Add olive oil, vinegar, Parmesan, wine, sugar and spices to bowl.
   Toss together and set aside.

3. Brush a thin layer of olive oil all over pizza crust.

   Scatter with mozzarella, then bake in preheated **oven** directly on center rack, for 10 minutes or until pizza is golden.

   ...meanwhile...
4. Rinse spinach in basket of salad spinner.
   Spin dry.
   Crumble feta cheese, slice strawberries, sliver onion and set out cashews, all in small serving dishes.

   Set out salad dressing.

   ...when timer rings for pizza crust...
5. Top hot pizza with bruschetta topping using a slotted spoon!

   If someone doesn't like tomatoes, pizza is the easiest thing to make two of...just change up the toppings! And it takes care of lunch the next day!

Ingredients:

Take out ingredients.

Bruschetta Topping
8 medium firm vine tomatoes (or 10 Roma tomatoes)
1 bunch green onion
  (approx 1 cup, finely chopped)
8 cloves fresh garlic, crushed
  I can't imagine bruschetta without garlic!

2 Tbsp olive oil, extra-virgin
1 Tbsp red wine vinegar
2 Tbsp Parmesan cheese, light, grated
1 Tbsp red wine
1 tsp sugar
1 tsp oregano
1 tsp basil leaves
16 twists fresh pepper

1 tsp olive oil, extra-virgin
12" pizza crust (1/2 lb or 225 g)
You want a nice soft white crust from the bakery section for this.
1/2 cup mozzarella cheese, part-skim, shredded (or cheddar cheese)

1 bag baby spinach (12 oz or 350 g)

1/4 cup feta cheese, light
8 strawberries
1/8 of a red onion
1/2 cup cashews, unsalted
1/3 cup favorite dressing, fat-free
  I like a creamy Vidalia onion dressing.

reserved bruschetta

Serves 4

DINNER IS READY IN 25 MINUTES

Equipment List:

Large mixing bowl
Cutting board
Stirring spoon
Salad spinner
Salad tongs
Small individual serving dishes
Slotted spoon
Sharp veggie knife
Garlic press
Pastry brush
Measuring cups and spoons
Cookie sheet

Per serving:

Calories	522
Fat	24.1 g
Protein	19.9 g
Carbohydrate	64.1 g
Fiber	9.8 g
Sodium	794 mg

U.S. Food Exchanges:		Cdn. Food Choices:	
3	Starch	2 1/2	Carb
2	Meat-med fat	2	Meat/Alt
3	Fat	3	Fat
2	Vegetable	1	Other Carb

20 to prep

WEEK 6

Steak with Peppercorn Brandy Sauce, Corn on the Cob and Mixed Greens

Instructions:

Don't change yet! Take out equipment.

1. Heat oil and butter in a large nonstick **fry pan** at medium-high.
   Brown each side of the steaks until they are almost cooked to your liking. *See page 32 for the steak doneness hand test.* **Remove from heat** and wrap steaks in foil to rest.

   Reduce heat to medium-low. Add garlic and peppercorns to the uncleaned pan and stir. Add brandy and stir. Gradually mix in flour, whisk in cream, then milk. Simmer until mixture thickens slightly. **Reduce heat** to a low simmer.

2. Place corn in a large **stove-top** pot. Add water, cover and bring to a boil. Once water boils, turn the corn and set timer for 5 minutes.

   ...meanwhile...
3. Rinse salad greens under cold water in a salad spinner. Spin dry. Place in salad bowl.
   Grate carrot over salad.
   Toss salad with salad dressing and toppings.

   ...when timer rings for corn...
4. Drain corn and then add butter and salt to pot. Swish the corn around to coat. Cover (no heat).
   If you like smoky flavors you can char the corn slightly by tossing it on the BBQ grill or under the broiler for a couple minutes.

5. Drain steak juice from foil into the peppercorn sauce. Whisk to combine.
   Serve sauce over steaks and enjoy!

Ingredients:

Take out ingredients.
1 Tbsp olive oil, extra-virgin
1 tsp butter
1 1/2 lbs or 675 g very thick top sirloin steaks, boneless and trimmed
aluminum foil

1 Tbsp fresh garlic (from a jar)
1 Tbsp mixed peppercorns
1 Tbsp brandy (or 1 Tbsp apple jelly)
2 tsp flour
1/2 cup 10% cream
2/3 cup 1% milk

4-6 cobs of corn (use frozen if not in season)
1 cup water

1 bag mixed salad greens (12 oz or 350 g)

1 carrot
1/3 cup favorite salad dressing, fat-free
Optional Toppings
blackberries, slivered red onion, nuts, etc.

1 tsp butter
1/4 tsp salt (optional)

Serves 4-6

35 MINUTES   READY, *LET'S EAT!*

Equipment List:

Large nonstick fry pan
Large stove-top pot w/lid
Colander
Salad spinner
Salad bowl
Salad tongs
Flipper
Stirring spoon
Whisk
Veggie grater
Measuring cups and spoons
Aluminum foil

Per serving:

Calories	342
Fat	11.7 g
Protein	30.4 g
Carbohydrate	30.6 g
Fiber	3.8 g
Sodium	254 mg

U.S. Food Exchanges:	Cdn. Food Choices:
1 Starch	1 1/2 Carb
3 1/2 Meat-very lean	3 1/2 Meat/Alt
1 Fat	1/2 Other Carb
1 Vegetable	
1/2 Milk-low fat	

WEEK 6

Quick Louisiana Gumbo with Rice and Broccoli

Instructions:

Don't change yet! Take out equipment.
1. Combine rice and water in a large microwave-safe pot with lid. **Microwave** at high 10 minutes, then medium 10 minutes. Remove from microwave and let stand.

2. Heat oil in a large **stove-top** pot over medium heat. Finely chop onion, adding to pot as you cut. Slice celery diagonally, adding to pot as you cut.
Add garlic and spices.

Add tomatoes and chicken broth, then stir.

Cut and add tomato.
Rinse okra and peppers in a colander, then stir into pot.
When mixture begins to boil, **reduce heat** to a high simmer.
Cut sausages into bite-size pieces, adding to pot as you cut.
Fold shrimp into gumbo.
Stir. Continue simmering until rice is ready.

3. Rinse broccoli in colander or steamer basket. Place water in the bottom of a **stove-top** pot and bring to a full boil with the broccoli in the basket above. Cover and set timer for 3 minutes…or microwave for the same amount of time. *See page 34.*
Toss with butter if you must.

Ingredients:

Take out ingredients.
1 1/2 cups basmati rice
3 cups water

1 tsp olive oil, extra-virgin
1 small red onion
2 ribs celery

1 Tbsp fresh garlic (from a jar)
1 1/2 tsp oregano
2 tsp Mrs. Dash Original seasoning
1/8 tsp cayenne pepper
3 Tbsp parsley flakes
2 bay leaves, dried (or use fresh)

1 can red pepper stewed tomatoes (19 oz or 540 mL)
2 cups chicken broth, reduced-sodium
1 firm vine-ripe tomato
1 pkg frozen cut okra (10 oz or 300 g)
1 cup frozen mixed bell peppers (or use fresh)

3 fully cooked and smoked turkey sausages (similar to pepperoni sticks)
1 lb or 450 g shrimp, large (deveined, cooked with tail on)

1 lb or 450 g broccoli florets
water

butter (optional)

<u>Serves 6</u>
Assumes one-fourth gumbo left over.

DINNER IS READY IN 30 MINUTES

Equipment List:

Large microwave-safe pot w/lid
Large stove-top pot
Stove-top pot w/steamer basket
Colander
2 cutting boards
Sharp veggie knife
Sharp meat knife
Can opener
2 stirring spoons
Measuring cups and spoons

Per serving:

Calories	409
Fat	4.2 g
Protein	27.6 g
Carbohydrate	71.2 g
Fiber	11.0 g
Sodium	656 mg

U.S. Food Exchanges:		Cdn. Food Choices:	
3	Starch	3	Carb
3	Meat-very lean	3	Meat/Alt
1	Vegetable	1	Other Carb
1/2	Other Carb		

Assumes one-fourth gumbo left over.

WEEK 6

Chicken en Croute
with Strawberry Skewers

Instructions:

...the night before...
Take out equipment.

1. Remove pastry from freezer and leave at room temperature until prep is done, then place in **fridge**.

2. Heat oil in a large nonstick **fry pan** at medium heat. Cut chicken into bite-size pieces, adding to pan as you cut. Stir until meat is no longer pink. Transfer to a medium bowl, cool, then cover and place in **fridge**.
...meanwhile...
Add gravy mix and curry powder to a small bowl or measuring cup. Gradually whisk in chicken broth.
Pour into an ice cube tray. Place in **freezer**.

3. Wash and finely chop green onions. Wash and slice mushrooms. Place in bowls in **fridge**.

...when you get home...
4. Preheat **oven** to **400° F**.
Cut the block of puff pastry into 4 equal squares. Roll each small square with a rolling pin or clean wine bottle, on a floured surface to approx 8" x 8".
Pile the following into the center of each pastry square: cooked chicken, magic cube, green onion, mushrooms, pepper and cheese.

Dip your fingers in water and run along the edge of pastry. Bring all four corners of the pastry to the top and pinch together. Pinch all four edges, starting from the peak down to the bottom, until all sides are sealed. Transfer to a cookie sheet and place in preheated **oven**. Set timer for 25 minutes. When pastry is golden brown they're ready.
...meanwhile...
5. Wash strawberries and thread onto skewers. Sprinkle cinnamon onto vanilla yogurt (for dipping). *You can also serve skewers on a green salad.*

Ingredients:

Take out ingredients.
1 block of puff pastry (7 oz or 200 g)
(pastry package may be 14 oz or 400 g containing 2 blocks; use only 1 block)

1 tsp canola oil
3 chicken breasts, boneless, skinless (1 lb or 450 g)

Magic Cubes
1 Tbsp dry gravy mix (for chicken)
I like Bisto.
1 tsp curry powder
1 can chicken broth, reduced-sodium (10 oz or 284 mL)

3 green onions
6 mushrooms

1 block defrosted puff pastry from fridge (4 servings)
flour
Filling for Each Pastry Square
1/2 cup cooked chicken
1 frozen magic cube
1 Tbsp green onion
1 1/2 mushrooms
pepper to taste
1 Tbsp cheddar cheese, light, shredded

water

20 strawberries
skewers
1 cup vanilla yogurt, light
cinnamon (optional)
green salad (optional)
Serves 4

DINNER IS READY IN 45 MINUTES

Equipment List:

...the night before...
Large nonstick fry pan
2 cutting boards
Medium-size mixing bowl w/lid
2 small mixing bowls
Meat knife & Veggie knife
Stirring spoon & Whisk
Ice cube tray & Can opener
Measuring cups and spoons
...when you get home...
Cookie sheet & Cutting board
Colander & Small mixing bowl
Veggie knife & Stirring spoon
Rolling pin & Serving plate
Measuring cups and spoons
Small dipping bowls & Skewers

Per serving:

Calories	452
Fat	17.1 g
Protein	37.0 g
Carbohydrate	36.5 g
Fiber	2.1 g
Sodium	538 mg

U.S. Food Exchanges:		Cdn. Food Choices:	
1	Starch	1 1/2	Carb
4 1/2	Meat-lean	4 1/2	Meat/Alt
1	Fat	1	Fat
1	Fruit	1	Fruit
1/2	Milk-low fat		

20 to prep

About the Recipes

Yellow

Any kind of fajita is a hit for my family. While working with a single dad on my show, I realized that by doubling this recipe he could serve two different meals by simply changing it up slightly. He could serve the first half on pasta and freeze the other half for fajitas in the future.

Vegetarians, load up on the veggies, lentils and beans and omit the beef.

Green

This meal is plain and simple, but I love the little cream sauce twist at the end. Some families couldn't get a blend of beans and carrots. Don't worry about it. Either put them together yourself or choose just one. The trick to doing this without having everything fall out is to start at one end. Try and tuck that cheese right in the middle. Whatever leaks out just adds to the flavor of the wine they are cooking in, which in turn adds to the flavor of the sauce.

Yellow

Once you've made homemade baked beans a few times, you just can't eat the canned ones. The homemade beans are firmer, which was something our test families mentioned, but began to appreciate. Man, these are so easy to freeze as well. I scoop 2 cup servings into freezer bags. Talk about a great quick side! …oooor for your adult children to steal out of the freezer when you aren't looking!!! Like we didn't notice!

Vegetarians, leave out the bacon.

Blue

Is this recipe a little finicky? Not if you have a BBQ grilling cage. You can bake these on the oven rack in the same way as on a BBQ grill (with foil underneath for the drippings.) When wings are prepared this way they are so much healthier than deep-fried wings, but just as crunchy and delicious. The sides make an interesting combination.

Vegetarians, leave out the wings. Add extra cheese and nuts to the mushrooms.

Red

Every family has one of those plain, old, ordinary meals that people crave… this is ours. It's very simple, but it's a staple meal in our home. I have avoided putting it in our books before, but then year after year we watched our kids' friends get hooked on it. You may find this meal sort of plain the first time, but every time you have it after, it's like a big hug!

If you are vegetarian and don't eat fish, replace the tuna with zucchini and sprinkle a little cheese on top.

Week 7

Yellow: Beef Fajita Stir-Fry on Pasta

> Our family rating: 10
> Your family rating: _____

Green: Chicken Cordon Bleu with Roasted Potatoes
               and Bean-Carrot Blend

> Our family rating: 9
> Your family rating: _____

Yellow: Maple Baked Beans with Multigrain Bread
               and Mixed Salad Greens

> Our family rating: 10
> Your family rating: _____

Blue: Garlic Chicken Wings, Portabella
               Mushrooms and Grilled Asparagus

> Our family rating: 10
> Your family rating: _____

Red: Tuna (or Chicken) Casserole
               with Rice and Broccoli

> Our family rating: 10
> Your family rating: _____

Beef Fajita Stir-Fry on Pasta

Instructions:

Don't change yet! Take out equipment.

1. Fill a large **stove-top** pot with water and bring to a boil for pasta.

2. Heat oil in a large nonstick **fry pan** or wok at medium-high. Slice onion, adding to pan as you cut. Sauté until translucent.
   Slice flank steak into thin strips, across the grain, adding to pan as you cut.
   Add garlic.
   Rinse, then sliver peppers, adding to pan as you slice.

   Add salsa, tomatoes, spices and ketchup to pan and mix.
   When sauce begins to boil, **reduce heat** to simmer.

   …meanwhile…

3. Add pasta to boiling water. Set timer to follow package directions (approx 11 minutes). Stir occasionally.
   …when timer rings…
   Rinse pasta in a colander under hot water.
   Return pasta to pot, no heat, and toss with a little olive oil and basil if you wish.

   To serve, sprinkle cheese over hot pasta, then spoon sauce onto cheese.
   Cilantro is optional. You either love it or you don't!!

   I like to make extra to use in fajita wraps another day!

Ingredients:

Take out ingredients.
water

1 tsp olive oil, extra-virgin
1 onion

1 1/2 lbs or 675 g flank steak, trimmed

2 tsp fresh garlic (from a jar)
1 red bell pepper
1/2 of a green bell pepper
1/2 of an orange or yellow bell pepper

1/2 cup chunky salsa
1 can Italian diced tomatoes
  (14 oz or 398 mL)
1 Tbsp chili powder
1 tsp ground cumin
2 Tbsp ketchup (or banana ketchup)

4 cups penne pasta

olive oil, extra-virgin (optional)
basil leaves (optional)

1/4 cup Tex-Mex cheese, shredded

cilantro (optional)

Serves 4-6

DINNER IS READY IN 25 MINUTES

Equipment List:

Large stove-top pot w/lid
Large nonstick fry pan or wok
Can opener
Colander
2 cutting boards
Sharp veggie knife
Sharp meat knife
2 stirring spoons
Measuring cups and spoons

Per serving:

Calories	496
Fat	8.7 g
Protein	36.5 g
Carbohydrate	66.0 g
Fiber	5.2 g
Sodium	376 mg

U.S. Food Exchanges:		Cdn. Food Choices:	
4	Starch	4	Carb
3 1/2	Meat-lean	3 1/2	Meat/Alt

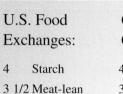

Chicken Cordon Bleu with Roasted Potatoes and Bean-Carrot Blend

Instructions:

Don't change yet! Take out equipment.

1. Preheat **oven** to **375° F**.
   Wash baby potatoes and place in a small oven-safe pan. Drizzle with olive oil and sprinkle with spice. Toss potatoes until well coated. Place in preheated **oven**.
   Set timer for 45 minutes.

2. Butterfly each chicken breast by slicing down the center of the thickest portion, BUT NOT ALL THE WAY THROUGH, the entire length of the breast. Open the split breast.
   Lay Swiss cheese on only half of the breast, then top with ham. Roll up breast starting with the cheese and ham side. Secure with a toothpick.

   Heat butter and oil in a large nonstick **fry pan** at medium.
   Sprinkle flour and paprika onto a piece of waxed paper and roll the breast until coated. Place in hot oil, and repeat, always starting with the coolest part of the pan first (usually the outside). Keep turning until all sides are brown. Transfer chicken to a dinner plate and let stand.
   Pour wine and chicken broth into the unclean pan and completely deglaze (get all the brown bits off of the bottom of the pan). Return chicken to pan.
   Cover and **reduce heat** to low, turning occasionally. Set timer for 25 minutes.

   ...meanwhile...

3. Rinse carrot-bean blend in colander or steamer basket. Place water in the bottom of a **stove-top** pot and bring to a full boil with the carrot-bean blend in the basket above. Cover and set timer for 5 minutes...or microwave for the same amount of time. *See page 34.*
   ...when timer rings for chicken...

4. Remove chicken from pan once again. Whisk cream and milk into pan. Return chicken to pan, and let simmer an additional 5 minutes. *Yum! Yum!*

Ingredients:

Take out ingredients.

20 baby potatoes (or cut up 4 large)
1 tsp olive oil, extra-virgin
1/2 tsp garlic & herb seasoning, salt-free

4 large chicken breasts, boneless, skinless (1 1/2 lbs or 675 g)
See page 33 for illustrations on how to butterfly a chicken breast.
6 thin slices Swiss cheese, light (2 oz or 60 g)
6 thin slices lean cooked ham (2 oz or 60 g)
I like Cajun-flavored ham.
6 toothpicks

1 tsp butter
1 tsp olive oil, extra-virgin
1/4 cup flour
1 Tbsp paprika
waxed paper

1/2 cup white wine
1 cup chicken broth, reduced-sodium
(can use a whole 10 oz or 284 mL can)

4 cups frozen carrot and bean blend (1 lb or 450 g)
1 cup water

1/2 cup 10% cream
1/4 cup 1% milk

Serves 4-6

DINNER IS READY IN 50 MINUTES

Equipment List:

Large nonstick fry pan w/lid
Stove-top pot w/steamer basket
Small oven-safe pan
Cutting board
Sharp meat knife
Flipper
Whisk
Dinner plate
Corkscrew for wine
Can opener
Measuring cups and spoons
Toothpicks
Waxed paper

Per serving:

Calories	389
Fat	8.2 g
Protein	37.8 g
Carbohydrate	39.8 g
Fiber	6.3 g
Sodium	319 mg

U.S. Food Exchanges:	Cdn. Food Choices:
2 Starch	2 Carb
4 1/2 Meat-very lean	4 1/2 Meat/Alt

Maple Baked Beans with Multigrain Bread and Mixed Salad Greens

Instructions:

...the night before...
Take out equipment.

1. Rinse beans in a colander, discarding shriveled ones. Place beans and water in a large **stove-top** pot at high heat. Finely chop onion, adding to pot as you cut. Stir. Bring to a full boil, then **reduce heat** to medium-low for a low boil. Set timer for 15 minutes.

   Combine brown sugar, maple syrup, pepper, mustard, Sambal Oelek, vinegar, molasses, ketchup and water in a large oven-safe pot or casserole. Trim and discard most of the fat from bacon.

   ...when timer rings for beans...
   Transfer beans, water and onion into the sauce pot and stir to combine. Lay bacon on top. Cover, let cool, then place in **fridge** overnight.

   ...in the morning...
2. Set **oven** to **250° F**. (Set at 225° F if gone more than 10 hours.)
   Place beans in **oven**.

   ...when you get home...
3. Reset **oven** to **350° F**.
   Remove 1 cup of beans with sauce into a bowl. Mash with a fork, return to bean pot and stir. Place beans back in **oven,** uncovered. Set timer for 20 minutes.

   ...when timer rings...
4. Place bread in **oven** next to beans, then **turn oven off**.

5. Rinse salad greens in basket of salad spinner and spin dry. Place on serving plates. Rinse strawberries, slice and place on greens. Drizzle salad dressing over greens and sprinkle with your favorite toppings.

Ingredients:

Take out ingredients.
1 1/4 cups dry white navy beans
5 cups water
1 onion

Sauce for Beans
1 Tbsp brown sugar
2 Tbsp maple syrup
1/2 tsp pepper
1/2 tsp Dijon mustard
1/2 tsp Sambal Oelek (crushed chili paste)
 (add more if you like it hot)
2 tsp vinegar
1/4 cup molasses
1/2 cup ketchup
1 cup water
4 bacon slices

NOTE
Homemade baked beans don't have the same mushy consistency as canned. They should be tender but firm. Once my kids were used to the change, they found the other "Yucky!" Those are their words.

2/3 loaf multigrain bread

1 bag mixed salad greens (12 oz or 350 g)
5 strawberries (or fruit in season)

1/3 cup salad dressing, poppy seed, light
Optional Toppings that we looove!
slivered red onion, feta, nuts...

Serves 6
Assumes one-fourth beans left over.

DINNER IS READY IN 20 MINUTES

Equipment List:

...the night before...
Large stove-top pot w/lid
Oven-safe pot or casserole w/lid
Colander
Cutting board
Large stirring spoon
Sharp meat & Veggie knives
Measuring cups and spoons
...when you get home...
Cutting board
Small mixing bowl
Salad spinner & Salad tongs
Bread knife & Veggie knife
Large stirring spoon & Fork
Measuring cups and spoons
Individual serving plates

Per serving:

Calories	406
Fat	10.8 g
Protein	14.8 g
Carbohydrate	66.4 g
Fiber	12.3 g
Sodium	646 mg

U.S. Food Exchanges:		Cdn. Food Choices:	
2	Starch	2	Carb
2	Meat-lean	2	Meat/Alt
1	Fat	1	Fat
1 1/2	Other Carb	1 1/2	Other Carb

Assumes one-fourth beans left over.

20 to prep

Garlic Chicken Wings, Portabella Mushrooms and Grilled Asparagus

Instructions:

Don't change yet! Take out equipment.
1. Preheat **BBQ grill** or grill pan to medium (approx **350° F**). *You can also use the oven.*

2. Spray a **BBQ grill cage** (or foil grill pan) with cooking spray. *If you don't have a cage, a foil grill pan works fine. The cage makes flipping easier.*
   Place wings in cage.
   Flip wings every 3-5 minutes. Set timer so you don't forget!
   ...meanwhile...

3. Brush the outside (smooth side) of each mushroom with olive oil.

   Spread the inside with chili sauce.
   Slice zucchini and sliver red onion. Layer zucchini, then red onion over chili sauce.
   Top with pineapple and sun-dried tomatoes.
   Sprinkle with spices.

   Drizzle balsamic vinegar over top, then sprinkle with Parmesan cheese, pine nuts and Gruyère cheese.
   Place mushrooms on individual pieces of aluminum foil sprayed with cooking spray.
   Cook 10-15 minutes on **BBQ grill** (place on outside corners of grill).
   ...meanwhile...

4. Transfer sauce from jar into a small bowl. Baste chicken wings with sauce, flipping cage each time you baste, until all sauce is used.

5. Snap off bottom nodes of asparagus and discard. Rinse asparagus, then place in **BBQ grill wok** or large stove-top fry pan at medium. Drizzle with olive oil and sprinkle with spice. Place on **BBQ grill** next to chicken. Toss regularly while continuing to baste wings.

6. Remove foil from bottom of mushrooms and cook mushrooms directly on **BBQ grill** for 2 minutes. YUM!!!

Ingredients:

Take out ingredients.

cooking spray

12-16 chicken wings (1 1/2 lbs or 675 g)

4 large portabella mushrooms (stems removed)
1 tsp olive oil, extra-virgin
4 Tbsp sweet Thai chili sauce
1 small zucchini (12-16 slices)
1/4 of a red onion
4 pineapple slices (fresh or canned)
1/4 cup sun-dried tomatoes (from a jar)
ground pepper to taste
2 tsp garlic & herb seasoning blend, salt-free

4 tsp balsamic vinegar
4 tsp Parmesan cheese, light, grated
4 Tbsp pine nuts
1/2 cup Gruyère cheese, shredded
aluminum foil
cooking spray

1 cup strong garlic spare-rib sauce
 (or use honey-garlic sauce recipe on page 74)

20 asparagus spears
You can lay asparagus across the grill if you don't have a BBQ wok or veggie pan.
1 tsp olive oil, extra-virgin
1 tsp Mrs. Dash Original seasoning

<u>**Serves 4-6**</u>

DINNER IS READY IN 40 MINUTES

Equipment List:

BBQ grill (or grill pan)
BBQ grill cage (or foil grill pan)
BBQ grill wok
  (or large stove-top fry pan)
Cutting board
Colander
Small bowl
Cheese grater
Sharp veggie knife
Flipper
2 basting brushes
Measuring cups and spoons
Aluminum foil

Per serving:

Calories	383
Fat	20.0 g
Protein	22.3 g
Carbohydrate	30.7 g
Fiber	3.9 g
Sodium	478 mg

20 to prep

U.S. Food Exchanges:		Cdn. Food Choices:	
1	Starch	1	Carb
3	Meat-mod fat	3	Meat/Alt
1	Fat	2	Fat
1	Other Carb	1	Other Carb

Assumes half spare-rib sauce wasted.

Tuna (or Chicken) Casserole with Rice and Broccoli

Instructions:

Don't change yet! Take out equipment.

1. Preheat **oven** to **350° F**.

Melt butter in a large **stove-top** pot at medium. **Remove from heat.** Whisk in flour and pepper until smooth.
Whisk milk gradually into flour mixture. Return **stove-top** pot to medium heat. Stir constantly until slightly thickened. **Remove from heat** and set aside.

Crumble crackers over bottom of an oven-safe casserole dish. Drain tuna, then crumble over crackers. Rinse and slice mushrooms, layering over tuna as you slice. Layer with peas, then pour sauce over top.

Top with a final layer of crumbled crackers. Cover and bake in preheated **oven**.
Set timer for 35 minutes.

...meanwhile...

2. Combine rice and water in a large microwave-safe pot with lid. **Microwave** at high 10 minutes, then medium 10 minutes.

3. Rinse broccoli in a colander or steamer basket. Place water in the bottom of a **stove-top** pot and bring to a boil with the broccoli in the basket above. Cover and set timer for 3 minutes...or microwave for the same amount of time. *See page 34.*
Toss with butter if you must.

...when timer rings for rice...
Lift rice with a fork and let rest.

My family loves to drizzle a little soy sauce over the rice. This is a huge family favorite. This meal seems plain at first, but the more you have it, the more it grows on you.

Ingredients:

Take out ingredients.

3 Tbsp butter
3 Tbsp flour
1/4 tsp pepper
2 cups 1% milk (approx)

3/4 cup stoned wheat crackers, crumbled, reduced-sodium (approx 15 small crackers)
1 can solid tuna or chicken in water, drained (6 1/2 oz or 184 g)
6 mushrooms
1 cup frozen baby peas
reserved sauce
3/4 cup stoned wheat crackers, crumbled, reduced-sodium (approx 15 small crackers)

1 1/2 cups basmati rice
3 cups water

1 lb or 450 g broccoli florets
water

butter (optional)

soy sauce, reduced-sodium (optional)

Serves 4-6

DINNER IS READY IN 30 MINUTES

Equipment List:

Large stove-top pot
Large oven-safe casserole w/lid
Large microwave-safe pot w/lid
Stove-top pot w/steamer basket
Cutting board
Large liquid measuring cup
Whisk
Can opener
Sharp veggie knife
Fork
Measuring cups and spoons

Per serving:

Calories	445
Fat	12.4 g
Protein	19.5 g
Carbohydrate	65.8 g
Fiber	4.8 g
Sodium	297 mg

U.S. Food Exchanges:		Cdn. Food Choices:	
3	Starch	4	Carb
1	Meat-lean	1	Meat/Alt
2	Fat	2	Fat
1	Vegetable		
1/2	Milk-low fat		

15
to
prep

About the Recipes

 Blue

This recipe is fabulous, easy and very gourmet. Most of our test families rated it 10 for weekday cooking. This is a great recipe to have in your back pocket after Thanksgiving or Christmas because it works great with turkey.
We tested this with mixed wild mushrooms for a vegetarian dish and found it absolutely amazing.

 **Yellow**

This soup is sooo delicious. I love that it only takes a couple of minutes to throw together the night before. When you get home the next day, the house smells amazing! As you may have noticed, I like to cook pasta separately when serving soup. When you put the pasta at the bottom of the bowl, then pour the soup over top, the noodles never get mushy.

Green

I love those little sesame-honey cookies, or whatever you call them, but I can never eat four and they are usually packaged that way. For some reason I looked at them one day and thought, I'm going to bake these on chicken. Don't ask me how my brain works, God only knows. Aaaanyway…my family and the test families give this a big thumbs up. I do want to point out that the sesame snaps never completely melt, so it's kind of like eating chicken with a crunchy top. It's fun!

 **Red**

This is one of my all-time-favorite nonjunk-junk foods. I hope it's yours. Remember, I always want the photograph to depict the way I eat the food. My family likes our steak medium-rare, but on the rare side. Cook the steak to your liking. It's a wow!
If you are vegetarian, rub a tiny bit of olive oil on red and yellow bell peppers, char them under the broiler and layer with sautéed mushrooms and your caramelized onions.

 **Yellow**

Just a caution, don't put your pan on too high or you will burn the outside of the fish before the inside is cooked. Remember to use your instant-read thermometer.
This recipe is great for vegetarians who eat fish. You can replace the fish with large slices of eggplant or zucchini. It's really yummy with the tartar sauce too! Replace the broccoli with edamame beans for more protein.

Week 8

Blue: **Chicken & Mushrooms in Pastry with Pesto-Glazed Veggies**

Our family rating: 9
Your family rating: _____

Yellow: **Easy Vegetable Minestrone Soup with Garlic Bread**

Our family rating: 9.5
Your family rating: _____

Green: **Sesame Snap Chicken with Pasta and Snap Peas**

Our family rating: 10
Your family rating: _____

Red: **Cajun Beefsteak with Cambozola, Berry au Jus and BLT Salad**

Our family rating: 9.5
Your family rating: _____

Yellow: **Pecan-Crusted Salmon, Sweet Potato Fries and Broccoli**

Our family rating: 8.5
Your family rating: _____

Chicken & Mushrooms in Pastry with Pesto-Glazed Veggies

Instructions:

Don't change yet! Take out equipment.
1. Preheat **oven** to **400° F**.

2. Melt butter in a medium **stove-top** pot on low heat. Wash and slice mushrooms, adding to pot as you cut. Stir and **remove from heat**.

Gradually whisk flour into pot until combined. Slowly whisk in chicken broth and milk. Return to heat and simmer on low. Stir in Worcestershire sauce and spice.

Remove meat from roaster chicken and cut into cubes. Add to sauce. Fold in peas.

...meanwhile...
2. Place pastry shells on a cookie sheet and bake in preheated **oven**. Set timer for 20 minutes.

3. Spray a large nonstick **fry pan** with cooking spray and heat at medium. Rinse peppers and zucchini and cut into large chunks, adding to pan as you cut. Dab with pesto and toss until tender.

4. When timer rings for pastry, remove from **oven**. Remove top center disk using a fork and set aside. Gently lift out the soft pastry from the inside of the shell and discard, leaving the bottom intact.

When you are ready to serve, place a shell on each plate and fill with sauce. Put a pastry disk on top of the sauce.

Serve alongside veggies.
YUUUUUUUMMMY...and it looks amazing,
so it's also a great entertaining dish.

Ingredients:

Take out ingredients.

2 Tbsp butter
10 mushrooms

2 Tbsp flour
1 cup chicken broth, reduced-sodium
1 cup 1% milk
1 tsp Worcestershire sauce
1 tsp Italian seasoning

2 cups cooked roaster chicken (from a deli)
1 cup frozen peas

1 pkg of 6 frozen puff pastry patty shells
  (10 oz or 300 g) *I like Tenderflake brand.*

cooking spray
1 red bell pepper
1 yellow bell pepper
2 medium zucchini
1 Tbsp basil pesto

Serves 4-6

DINNER IS READY IN 40 MINUTES

Equipment List:

Medium stove-top pot
Large nonstick fry pan
Cookie sheet
2 cutting boards
Stirring spoon
Can opener
Whisk
Flipper
Sharp meat knife
Sharp veggie knife
Fork
Measuring cups and spoons

Per serving:

Calories	396
Fat	21.2 g
Protein	21.0 g
Carbohydrate	31.1 g
Fiber	2.9 g
Sodium	364 mg

U.S. Food Exchanges:		Cdn. Food Choices:	
2	Starch	2	Carb
3	Meat-lean	3	Meat/Alt
2	Fat	2	Fat

20 to prep

Easy Vegetable Minestrone Soup with Garlic Bread

Instructions:

...the night before...
Take out equipment.

1. Heat oil in a large **stove-top** pot at medium-high. Finely chop onion, adding to pot as you cut. Sauté until translucent and just slightly browned. Remove from heat and toss into crock of **slow cooker**. Slice celery and carrots thinly, adding to crock as you cut. Add garlic.

   Add vegetable broth, wine, tomatoes, beans, tomato paste, spices, Parmesan cheese and pesto to pot. Stir to combine.

   Cover and place in **fridge** overnight.

...in the morning...
2. Return crock, with lid, to the **slow cooker** and set on **low heat**.

...when you get home...
3. Preheat **oven** to 350° F.

4. Fill a large **stove-top** pot with water for pasta. Cover and bring to a boil.
   ...meanwhile...
5. Slice bread lengthwise, lightly butter and sprinkle with garlic powder and parsley. Place bread directly on center rack of **oven**, butter side up, then **turn oven off**!

6. Place pasta in boiling water. Set timer for 7 minutes or follow package directions for al dente pasta.
   When timer rings for pasta, rinse in a colander under hot water and return to pot, **no heat**. Toss with a little olive oil if you like.

   Serve pasta in the bottom of each bowl and pour hot soup over top. YUUMMMM!!!!
   Don't forget to take the bread out!

Ingredients:

Take out ingredients.
1 tsp canola oil
1 large onion

2-3 ribs celery
2-3 carrots
2 tsp fresh garlic (from a jar)

3 1/2 - 4 cups vegetable broth, reduced-sodium
1 cup white wine (can use nonalcoholic or water)
1 can diced tomatoes (14 oz or 398 mL)
1 can mixed beans (19 oz or 540 mL)
2 Tbsp tomato paste
2 tsp Italian seasoning
1/8 tsp fresh pepper
1/4 cup Parmesan cheese, grated, light
1/4 cup basil pesto (from a jar)

water

1 French loaf or baguette
2 Tbsp butter (1 Tbsp per side)
1/2 tsp garlic powder
1/2 tsp parsley flakes

2 cups fusilli pasta

1 tsp olive oil, extra-virgin (optional)

<u>Serves 8</u>
If you have a smaller family, the leftovers freeze great!

DINNER IS READY IN 25 MINUTES

Equipment List:

…the night before…
Slow cooker
Large stove-top pot
Cutting board
Sharp veggie knife
Stirring spoon
Corkscrew for wine
Can opener
Measuring cups and spoons
…when you get home…
Large stove-top pot w/lid
Colander
Cutting board & Bread knife
Butter knife or spreader
Stirring spoon & Soup ladle
Measuring cups and spoons

Per serving:

Calories	421
Fat	10.4 g
Protein	16.5 g
Carbohydrate	66.2 g
Fiber	9.1 g
Sodium	1153 mg

U.S. Food Exchanges:		Cdn. Food Choices:	
3	Starch	4	Carb
1	Meat-lean	1	Meat/Alt
1/2	Fat	1 1/2	Fat
2	Vegetable		

WEEK 8

Sesame Snap Chicken
with Pasta and Snap Peas

Instructions:

Don't change yet! Take out equipment.

1. Preheat **oven** to **400° F**.

   Spray a large oven-safe pan with cooking spray. Place chicken thighs in pan and drizzle with soy sauce. Flip with a fork until well coated, then flatten into a single layer.

   Sprinkle with ginger and garlic. Finely chop cilantro and sprinkle over thighs. Place a sesame snap on top of each thigh.
   Place in preheated **oven**. Set timer for 20 minutes.

2. Rinse snap peas in a colander and add to a large nonstick **fry pan** (no heat). Drizzle with sesame oil and sprinkle with cashews. Let stand.

   ...when timer rings for chicken...

3. Leave chicken in the oven and **reduce heat** to **350° F**. Reset timer for 12 minutes.

4. Fill a large **stove-top** pot with water, cover and bring to a boil.

5. Heat veggies in **fry pan** at medium, tossing occasionally.

6. Place pasta in boiling water. Set timer according to package directions minus 1 minute.
   ...when timer rings for pasta...
   Rinse pasta in colander and set aside (leave in the colander). Add chicken broth, curry and honey to uncleaned pasta pot and bring to a boil. Return pasta to pot and **turn heat off**. Gently toss to coat pasta. Cover to keep hot until chicken is ready.

   Snap peas are ready when tender but crunchy. The sesame snaps are not supposed to completely melt. This chicken is crunchy and fun!

Ingredients:

Take out ingredients.

cooking spray
8 large chicken thighs, boneless, skinless
  (1 3/4 lbs or 800 g)
1 Tbsp soy sauce, reduced-sodium

1 tsp ginger powder (for all)
1 tsp garlic powder (for all)
2 Tbsp cilantro (optional)
8 sesame snaps (sesame-honey crisps found in candy aisle)

1 lb or 450 g snap peas
1/2 tsp sesame oil
1/4 cup cashews, unsalted (optional)

water

3/4 lb or 350 g spaghetti pasta
  (or use steam-fried egg noodles as shown; they are higher in fat, but a nice change)

1 cup chicken broth, reduced-sodium
2 tsp curry powder
1 Tbsp liquid honey

<u>Serves 4-6</u>

45 MINUTES   READY, *LET'S EAT!*

Equipment List:

Large oven-safe pan
Large nonstick fry pan
Large stove-top pot w/lid
Cutting board
Colander
Sharp veggie knife
2 stirring spoons
Can opener
Fork
Measuring cups and spoons

Per serving:

Calories	478
Fat	9.7 g
Protein	35.2 g
Carbohydrate	59.9 g
Fiber	2.1 g
Sodium	321 mg

U.S. Food Exchanges:		Cdn. Food Choices:	
3	Starch	3	Carb
4	Meat-lean	4	Meat/Alt
2	Vegetable	1	Other Carb

Cajun Beefsteak with Cambozola, Berry au Jus and BLT Salad

Instructions:

Don't change yet! Take out equipment.

1. Preheat **oven** to **350° F**.
   Slice off both ends of French loaf so you have straight edges. *I pop these in the freezer for garlic bread another time.* Slice loaf down the center lengthwise. On the top half only, smear on the Cambozola cheese. Butter the bottom half, then sprinkle with garlic powder and parsley. Place both sides in **oven**, butter or cheese side up, then TURN OVEN OFF.

2. Heat oil in a large nonstick **fry pan** at medium heat. Sliver onion, tossing into pan as you cut. Stir until caramelized and sweet. Sprinkle with spice. Remove from pan and set aside in bowl.

   Spice both sides of steak, then place in the uncleaned onion pan at medium.

   …meanwhile…
   Pour beef broth into a small **stove-top** pot at high heat. Add jam and paprika. Stir. Bring to a boil while stirring, then **reduce heat** to simmer.

   When steaks are browned, flip to cook other side.

3. Rinse lettuce in basket of salad spinner. Spin dry. Arrange on serving plates. Finely chop tomato. Crumble feta on top. Crumble bacon on top. Drizzle with dressing.

4. When steaks are cooked to your desired doneness, let rest on a plate. *See page 32.* Pour jus into steak **fry pan**, then stir to get all the little bits off the bottom (called deglazing). Simmer at the lowest heat.

   Slice meat into very thin strips. Stack onto one side of bread. Top with onion. Sandwich with the other side, then slice into strips.
   Serve beside salad with a small bowl of jus.

Ingredients:

Take out ingredients.

1 French loaf
1/4 cup Cambozola cheese (or Gorgonzola or grated Gruyère) *Cambozola cheese is milder than blue cheese and it's creamy, making it easy to spread.*
1 Tbsp butter
2 tsp garlic powder
1 tsp parsley flakes

1 tsp canola oil
1 onion
1 tsp chipotle seasoning, salt-free

1 tsp peppercorn blend or steak spice, salt-free
1 1/2 lbs or 675 g top sirloin or tenderloin steak, 2 inches thick, boneless, trimmed

Berry au Jus
1 can beef broth, reduced-sodium (10 oz or 284 mL)
1 Tbsp berry jam (three-fruit blend)
1 tsp paprika

1 bag Romaine lettuce (12 oz or 350 g)
1 firm tomato
2 Tbsp feta cheese, crumbled, low-fat (optional)
4 slices fully cooked bacon (purchase this way)
1/3 cup ranch or blue cheese dressing, fat-free (or your favorite)

If you don't think the kids will want it as a sandwich, slice off their bread before stacking with meat and serve the meat and bread as separate components with the salad.
Serves 4-6

30 MINUTES   READY, *LET'S EAT!*

Equipment List:

Large nonstick fry pan
Small stove-top pot
2 cutting boards
Salad spinner
Salad tongs
Small bowl
Sharp veggie knife
Sharp meat knife
Bread knife
Butter knife or spreader
2 stirring spoons
Flipper
Can opener
Measuring cups and spoons
Individual serving plates

Per serving:

Calories	454
Fat	15.7 g
Protein	30.9 g
Carbohydrate	46.5 g
Fiber	4.1 g
Sodium	907 mg

U.S. Food Exchanges:		Cdn. Food Choices:	
2	Starch	3	Carb
3	Meat-lean	3 1/2	Meat/Alt
2	Fat	1	Fat
2	Vegetable		

Assumes one-seventh
French bread left over.

Pecan-Crusted Salmon, Sweet Potato Fries and Broccoli

Instructions:

Don't change yet! Take out equipment.
1. Preheat **oven** to **450° F**.
   Drizzle oil onto a cookie sheet with sides and heat for 30 seconds in the oven.
   Remove pan from oven, scatter fries on pan in a single layer and return to oven. Set timer for 10 minutes. Toss and reset for an additional 10 minutes, or follow package directions.
   …meanwhile…
2. Combine mayonnaise, spices, lemon juice and relish together in a small mixing bowl.
   Set aside in **fridge**.
   I love tartar sauce!

3. Place flour on a large piece of waxed paper.
   Pour water into a small bowl.

   Combine pecans and bread crumbs on a different large piece of waxed paper.
   Finely chop shallot and add to bread crumb mixture. Add ginger, salt and pepper.
   Combine well with a fork.

   Spray a large nonstick **fry pan** with cooking spray and heat at medium.
   Dunk each fillet into the flour, then water, then pecan coating. *Pick up the sides of waxed paper and lift back and forth to coat fillets in both the flour and crumb mixture.*
   Sauté for approx 3 minutes. Spray the top of the salmon with cooking spray, turn and sauté other side for approx 3 minutes.
   …meanwhile…
4. Rinse broccoli in colander or steamer basket. Place water in the bottom of a **stove-top** pot and bring to a full boil with the broccoli in the basket above. Cover and set timer for 3 minutes…or microwave for the same amount of time. *See page 34.* Toss with butter if you must.

Ingredients:

Take out ingredients.

1 Tbsp canola oil

4-6 cups sweet potato fries (or regular fries)

<u>Optional Tartar Sauce</u>
1/2 cup mayonnaise, light
1 tsp Mrs. Dash Original seasoning
dash of cayenne
dash of lemon pepper
2 tsp lemon juice
3 tsp sweet green relish
1/2 - 1 tsp hot pepper relish (optional)

1/2 cup flour
waxed paper
water
1/2 cup crushed pecans *If you can't buy crushed pecans, wrap pecans in a clean dish towel and smash with a mallet.*
1 cup fine bread crumbs
waxed paper
1 shallot
3 Tbsp fresh ginger (from a jar)
pinch of salt & pepper
cooking spray

1 1/2 lbs or 675 g salmon fillets, skinless, boneless (4-6 equal parts)
flour, water, reserved crumb mixture

cooking spray

1 lb or 450 g broccoli florets
water

butter (optional)
<u>Serves 4-6</u>

25 MINUTES   READY, *LET'S EAT!*

Equipment List:

Cookie sheet with sides
Large nonstick fry pan
Stove-top pot w/steamer basket
Cutting board
Colander
2 small bowls
Mallet
Stirring spoon
Flipper
Sharp veggie knife
Fork
Measuring cups and spoons
Clean dish towel
Waxed paper

Per serving:

Calories	428
Fat	14.4 g
Protein	30.5 g
Carbohydrate	45.2 g
Fiber	4.7 g
Sodium	325 mg

U.S. Food Exchanges:		Cdn. Food Choices:	
2	Starch	2 1/2	Carb
3	Meat-lean	3	Meat/Alt
1	Fat	1	Fat
2	Vegetable		

20
to
prep

About the Recipes

Red

This pasta is really different and amazing no matter what you take out or put in. If you don't like sun-dried tomatoes, take them out and add zucchini. It's the sauce that makes it unique.

If you are vegetarian, you can load up on more veggies and throw in some frozen podded edamame beans for extra protein.

Green

I was making Thai and pepperoni pizzas for a treat night. I was sure I had pepperoni in the freezer when doing my meal plan, so I crossed it off the list, but the nonexistent pepperoni ghost ate it all (need I say more?). One of our kids isn't crazy about Thai pizza, so I threw the leftover taco sauce on top of a crust with some toppings and the kids flipped out over it.

Vegetarians can use soy grind instead of ground beef and you'd never know the difference.

Yellow

This salmon recipe has shocked many parents. Their kids who didn't eat fish liked it! Some of our test families found the grapefruit too strong a flavor, so they replaced them with large oranges. Go for it!

If you are a vegetarian who eats fish—great, otherwise you are on your own.

Yellow

When we think chili we usually think beef, but not this time. You would never know this chili is made with turkey. Adding a bit of maple syrup and bacon gives it a nice little unexpected twist.

Vegetarians can use veggie hamburger replacement and tofu bacon. Yum!

Blue

This started as a crown roast on my show, but was difficult to find in most grocery stores so I started experimenting. I took boneless chops, laid them over the stuffing and *voilà*! The cooking time was reduced to an hour, aaand it looks beautiful. The stuffing is delicious. If you love applesauce on your pork, like we do, I suggest you get the single-serve variety. That way you use only what you need. This is a great entertaining dish.

Week 9

Red: Chicken & Sun-Dried Tomato Pasta
with Broccoli

Our family rating: 9.5
Your family rating: _____

Green: Taco Pizza with Melon Salad

Our family rating: 10
Your family rating: _____

Yellow: Sesame-Crusted Salmon, Sour Cream
Mashed Potatoes and Fruit Salad

Our family rating: 9
Your family rating: _____

Yellow: Canadian Maple Turkey Chili
with Fresh Veggies

Our family rating: 8.5
Your family rating: _____

Blue: Apple-Cinnamon Pork Chops with
Cranberry-Rice Stuffing and Carrots

Our family rating: 9.5
Your family rating: _____

Chicken & Sun-Dried Tomato Pasta
with Broccoli

Instructions:

Don't change yet! Take out equipment.
1. Fill a large **stove-top** pot with water, cover and bring to a boil.

2. Heat oil in a large nonstick **fry pan** at medium-high. Sliver onion, adding to pan as you cut. Stir occasionally, until onion becomes translucent and begins to turn a caramel color.

    Cut chicken into bite-size pieces and gradually add to pan as you cut. Toss until chicken is no longer pink.
    Cut bacon into chunks, adding to pan as you cut.
    Chop celery coarsely and slice mushrooms, adding to pan as you cut. Add sun-dried tomatoes, lemon juice, curry paste, wine, dressing and milk to pan. Stir to combine. **Reduce heat** to low, stirring occasionally.

    ...meanwhile...
3. Place pasta in boiling water, stir and cook uncovered. Set timer according to package directions, approx 8 minutes.

4. Rinse broccoli in colander or steamer basket. Place water in the bottom of a **stove-top** pot and bring to a full boil with the broccoli in the basket above. Cover and set timer for 3 minutes...or microwave for the same amount of time. *See page 34.* Toss with butter if you must.

    ...when timer rings for pasta...
5. Rinse the pasta under hot water in a colander. Let drain and return to pasta pot. Toss with a little olive oil if you like and sprinkle with a little dried basil. *That's what we do!*

    Dinner is ready!

Ingredients:

Take out ingredients.
water

1 tsp olive oil, extra-virgin
1 onion

3 chicken breasts, boneless, skinless
 (1 lb or 450 g)

4 strips precooked bacon (from a box)
 (or use turkey bacon)
1 large celery rib
7 mushrooms
2 Tbsp sun-dried tomatoes (from a jar)
1 Tbsp lemon juice
1-2 tsp Madras curry paste
1/4 cup white wine (can be nonalcoholic)
1/4 cup poppy seed salad dressing, light
1 1/2 cups 1% milk

spaghetti pasta (12 oz or 350 g)

1 lb or 450 g broccoli florets
1 cup water

1 tsp butter (optional)

1 tsp olive oil, extra-virgin (optional)
1/2 tsp dried basil leaves (optional)

Serves 4-6

25 MINUTES   READY, *LET'S EAT!*

Equipment List:

Large stove-top pot w/lid
Stove-top pot w/steamer basket
Large nonstick fry pan
Colander
2 cutting boards
Sharp meat knife
Sharp veggie knife
2 stirring spoons
Corkscrew for wine
Measuring cups and spoons

Per serving:

Calories	387
Fat	7.6 g
Protein	30.3 g
Carbohydrate	49.2 g
Fiber	2.1 g
Sodium	299 mg

15 to prep

U.S. Food Exchanges:		Cdn. Food Choices:	
2	Starch	3	Carb
3	Meat-lean	3	Meat/Alt
1/2	Milk-low fat		
2	Vegetable		

WEEK 9

Taco Pizza with Melon Salad

Instructions:

Don't change yet! Take out equipment.

1. Preheat **oven** to **350° F**.
   Brown ground beef in large nonstick **fry pan** at medium-high. Add spices while meat is browning, stirring occasionally.

   When meat is no longer pink, add ketchup, salsa and water. **Reduce heat** to simmer. Meat mixture will thicken within 10 minutes.

   ...meanwhile...

2. Wash and finely chop green onion and tomatoes. Rinse and chop cilantro. Set these aside for toppings.

3. Brush a thin layer of olive oil all over crust. Spread meat mixture over crust. Layer with your favorite toppings.
   Top with shredded mozzarella cheese.

   Bake in preheated **oven** for 10 minutes or until crust is browned.

4. Rinse lettuce. Separate onto individual serving plates. Scrub outside of cantaloupe or mango, then peel and cut into bite-size pieces. Sliver red onion thinly and layer on top. Sprinkle with croutons and drizzle with salad dressing.

   When timer rings for pizza, you may like to broil the cheese a little more. Don't do this unless you are babysitting it, though, as there is nothing worse than charred pizza. I've been there!

   Serve pizza with sides of salsa, sour cream and chilies...yum yum yum!

Ingredients:

Take out ingredients.

1/2 lb or 225 g ground beef, extra-lean
1 tsp chili powder
1 tsp onion flakes
1/2 tsp ground cumin
1/8 tsp turmeric

1/4 cup ketchup
1/4 cup chunky salsa
1/4 cup water

2 green onions
2 Roma tomatoes
1/4 cup cilantro

1 tsp olive oil, extra-virgin
12" thin-crust pizza base (1/2 lb or 225 g)
reserved meat mixture
1 cup mozzarella cheese, part-skim, shredded

1 head green leaf lettuce
1 small cantaloupe or mango
1/8 of a red onion
1/2 cup croutons
1/3 cup salad dressing, fat-free
I like Vidalia onion.

Optional Toppings
salsa, sour cream, hot chili flakes

Serves 4

35 MINUTES   READY, *LET'S EAT!*

Equipment List:

Large nonstick fry pan
Small serving bowls
Cutting board
Colander
Salad spinner
Salad tongs
Pastry brush
Stirring spoon
Pizza cutter
Sharp veggie knife
Measuring cups and spoons
Individual serving plates
Cookie sheet

Per serving:

Calories	466
Fat	15.8 g
Protein	25.4 g
Carbohydrate	58.5 g
Fiber	5.9 g
Sodium	1057 mg

U.S. Food Exchanges:		Cdn. Food Choices:	
2 1/2	Starch	3	Carb
3	Meat-lean	3	Meat/Alt
2	Fat	2	Fat
1	Fruit	1/2	Other Carb

15 to prep

W
E
E
K

9

Sesame-Crusted Salmon, Sour Cream Mashed Potatoes and Fruit Salad

Instructions:

Don't change yet! Take out equipment.

1. Preheat **oven** to **425° F**.

2. Cut potatoes into quarters and place in **stove-top** pot as you cut. Rinse, then cover with cold water. Bring to a boil, then **reduce heat** to a low boil.

   ...meanwhile...

3. Combine soy sauce, mustard and honey in a small bowl.

   Spray an oven-safe pan with cooking spray. Rinse salmon under cold water and pat dry with paper towels. Score the thickest part of the salmon, then place in pan. *See page 30.* Drizzle salmon sauce on top of each piece. Generously scatter sesame seeds on top of each piece. Place salmon in preheated **oven** for 8 to 10 minutes, or until cooked through.

   ...while salmon and potatoes are cooking...

4. Cut grapefruit in half. Hollow out each half and place fruit in a medium bowl.
   Wash, peel and slice melon into small chunks and add to bowl. Wash and slice strawberries, adding to bowl as you cut. Wash grapes and add to bowl.
   Stir together and use to fill hollowed grapefruit halves.
   Top with yogurt.

5. When a knife easily slides through a potato, **turn heat off**.
   Drain potatoes. Whip or mash in the following ingredients: sour cream, milk, butter, garlic, pepper and parsley. *I like to whip my potatoes with an electric beater.*

   Note: I always like to make extra mashed potatoes to have on hand. Simply place in an airtight bag or container and freeze. When ready to use them, defrost, warm in microwave and whip them again with a drizzle of milk.

Ingredients:

Take out ingredients.

4-6 large thin-skinned potatoes
  (2 lbs or 900 g)
water

Salmon Sauce
2 Tbsp soy sauce, reduced-sodium
2 tsp mustard
2 Tbsp liquid honey

cooking spray
6 salmon fillets, boneless, skinless
  (1 1/2 lbs or 675 g)
paper towels

1/2 cup toasted sesame seeds

2-3 grapefruit (or large oranges)

1 small melon of choice
  (cantaloupe, honeydew, etc.)
8 strawberries
2 cups red seedless grapes

French vanilla yogurt (optional)

1/2 cup sour cream, reduced-fat
1/2 cup 1% milk
2 Tbsp butter
4 tsp fresh garlic (in a jar)
1 tsp pepper
2 tsp parsley flakes

Serves 4-6

30 MINUTES   READY, *LET'S EAT!*

Equipment List:

Large stove-top pot w/lid
Oven-safe pan
Colander
Cutting board
Medium mixing bowl
Small mixing bowl
Potato masher
2 stirring spoons
Sharp veggie knife
Sharp meat knife
Butter knife
Spoon
Measuring cups and spoons
Paper towels

Per serving:

Calories	519
Fat	17.2 g
Protein	31.4 g
Carbohydrate	64.0 g
Fiber	7.8 g
Sodium	364 mg

U.S. Food Exchanges:		Cdn. Food Choices:	
2	Starch	3	Carb
3	Meat-lean	3	Meat/Alt
2	Fat	2	Fat
1	Fruit	1	Fruit
1/2	Milk-low fat		

20
to
prep

Canadian Maple Turkey Chili with Fresh Veggies

Instructions:

...the night before...

Take out equipment.

1. Heat oil in a large **stove-top** pot at medium. Sliver onion, adding to pot as you cut. Cook until onion is soft and slightly translucent, stirring occasionally. Cut bacon into chunks and add to pot. Add ground turkey, stirring until no longer pink. Add maple syrup. Transfer to center crock of **slow cooker**. Wash and cut celery into chunks, then slice mushrooms, adding to crock as you cut. Wash, then coarsely chop peppers and tomato, adding to crock as you chop.

   Add spices, tomato soup, baked beans and ketchup. Drain and rinse mixed beans and add. Mix in carrots and green beans.

   Stir to combine, cover and place in **fridge** overnight.

...in the morning...

2. Return center crock with lid to **slow cooker** and set at **low heat**.

...just before dinner...

3. Add corn to chili. Stir to combine.

4. Rinse veggies and arrange on a plate with dip.

Serve with whole-wheat rolls if you wish.

Ingredients:

Take out ingredients.

1 tsp canola oil
1 onion

6 slices fully cooked bacon (buy this way)
1 lb or 450 g ground turkey
2 Tbsp maple syrup

2 ribs of celery
10 mushrooms
1/2 of a green bell pepper
1/2 of a red bell pepper
1 large tomato

1 Tbsp chili powder
1 Tbsp ground cumin
1/8 tsp each salt and pepper
1/8 tsp cayenne (optional)
1 can tomato soup, reduced-sodium
   (10 oz or 284 mL)
1 can baked beans in tomato sauce
   (14 oz or 398 mL)
1/2 cup ketchup
1 can mixed beans (19 oz or 540 mL)
   (kidney, garbanzo, combinations vary)
1 cup frozen baby carrots
1 cup frozen or fresh green beans

If you need to cook this for more than 6 hours, add an additional cup of water.
Read about slow cookers on page 31.

1 cup frozen corn

1 package of cut-up raw veggies
   (1 lb or 450 g): broccoli, cauliflower...
1/2 cup ranch dressing, fat-free

6-8 whole-wheat rolls (optional)

<u>**Serves 6-8**</u>

30 MINUTES   READY, *LET'S EAT!*

Equipment List:

...the night before...
Slow cooker
Large stove-top pot
Cutting board
Sharp meat knife
Sharp veggie knife
Can opener
Stirring spoon
Measuring cups and spoons
...just before dinner...
Colander
Small serving bowl
Stirring spoon
Measuring cups
Serving plate

Per serving:

Calories	386
Fat	8.8 g
Protein	24.4 g
Carbohydrate	57.8 g
Fiber	11.3 g
Sodium	1013 mg

U.S. Food Exchanges:		Cdn. Food Choices:	
2	Starch	2	Carb
2 1/2	Meat-mod fat	2 1/2	Meat/Alt
1	Other Carb	1/2	Fat
		1	Other Carb

20 to prep

WEEK 9

Apple-Cinnamon Pork Chops
with Cranberry-Rice Stuffing and Carrots

Instructions:

Don't change yet! Take out equipment.

1. Spray a large nonstick **fry pan** (or electric fry pan) with cooking spray and set heat at medium-high. Sprinkle garlic powder, pepper and salt over one side of the chops. Sauté chops spice side down until browned, approx 2 minutes.

   Spice other side of chops, then flip to brown that side. Transfer chops to a plate, but do not wash the pan.
   Preheat **oven** to **425° F.**

2. Melt butter and olive oil together in the uncleaned **fry pan** at medium-low. Finely chop onion and celery, adding to pan as you cut. Slice mushrooms, adding to pan as you slice.

   Add rice, spices, broth and craisins. Bring to a boil, then **remove from heat**.
   Fold in bread crumbs. Stir to combine.

   Spray a large lasagna or cake pan with cooking spray. Scoop 6 mounds of stuffing onto pan.

3. Press a chop onto each mound of rice stuffing. Wash and slice apples into quarters. Remove core from each, then slice into thin slivers. Arrange apple slices all over chops. Sprinkle with brown sugar and cinnamon. Bake in preheated **oven**. Set timer for 40 minutes.

4. Place baby carrots in a different oven-safe casserole. Drizzle with olive oil and spice. Toss to coat and place in **oven** to cook alongside chops.

   ...when timer rings...
   Remove chops and cover with a lid or foil. (Instant-read thermometer will read **170° F.**)
   Turn oven off but leave carrots in until ready to serve.

Ingredients:

Take out ingredients.
olive oil cooking spray

1 tsp garlic powder
1/2 tsp pepper
pinch of salt
6 thick pork loin chops, boneless, trimmed (2 lbs or 900 g)
1 tsp garlic powder
1/2 tsp pepper
pinch of salt

Cranberry-Rice Stuffing
1/2 tsp butter
1/2 tsp olive oil
1/2 of an onion
1 rib of celery
5 mushrooms
1 cup white and wild rice blend
  I like Canoe brand.
1/2 tsp poultry seasoning
1/2 tsp oregano
2 cups chicken broth, reduced-sodium
1/2 cup craisins or raisins
2 cups large bread crumbs
olive oil cooking spray

2-3 large Spartan or Macintosh apples

2 tsp brown sugar
1 tsp cinnamon

4 cups baby carrots
1-2 tsp olive oil
1 tsp marjoram (or use basil leaves)

This is such an easy down-home meal; bonus: it's hands free while you are walking the dog or playing with your kids, and it's YUUUUUMMMY!
Serves 6
Assumes one-sixth stuffing left over.

60 MINUTES   READY, *LET'S EAT!*

Equipment List:

Large nonstick fry pan w/lid
  (or electric fry pan w/lid)
Large lasagna or cake pan
Medium oven-safe casserole
  w/lid
Cutting board
Flipper
2 stirring spoons
Instant-read thermometer
Sharp veggie knife
Can opener
Measuring cups and spoons
Serving plate
Aluminum foil

Per serving:

Calories	415
Fat	5.9 g
Protein	39.3 g
Carbohydrate	50.4 g
Fiber	5.0 g
Sodium	694 mg

U.S. Food Exchanges:		Cdn. Food Choices:	
2	Starch	2	Carb
4	Meat-very lean	4	Meat/Alt
1/2	Fruit	1	Other Carb
1	Vegetable		

Assumes one-sixth stuffing left over.

20 to prep

About the Recipes

 Green

When making this recipe, remember it's really important to put the Parmesan on top of the meat before you put the sauce over top. You will finish it up with some more Parmesan later, but you want that Parm flavor to cook right through the meat.

If you are vegetarian, this is sooo good with eggplant. My only suggestion is to sprinkle cornflake crumbs over the Parm before you put the sauce over top.

 Yellow

Killer—yummy—yummy! This is a really nice creamy and flavorful curry, and it's very mild for the average person. You can replace the pork with chicken if you like.

If you are making this dish vegetarian, you need to first fry up your firm tofu, then follow the instructions as if you were using pork.

 Red

This originated with eating an Asian salmon tartare at a restaurant. I loved the flavors but wanted to create a more family-friendly version. The families we tested said the first one they ate was good, but then they wanted another and another. That's what we found as well. They are addictive. This is meant to be a fun, light dinner. I have this on one of our family movie nights so that my waistline doesn't suffer from eating popcorn later on.

If you are vegetarian, soak firm tofu in the dressing for a bit, before tossing in the coleslaw, so it takes on the flavor of the dressing.

 Blue

Just a tip, when doing this recipe I chop my leeks and bag them the night before. The only reason I do this is because it's a little finicky washing the sand from every layer. It's kind of a weird recipe in that the flavor doesn't taste like a bunch of leeks. In fact, two onion haters I know went back for seconds (leeks are part of the onion family). This is an amazing entertaining dish! Vegetarians can leave out the chicken.

Red

Do you notice a little theme in this last week? Entertaining! I can't even count the number of people who have claimed they hate lamb (YOLANDA) until I teach them how to cook a rack properly. The trick is to use wonderful spices or a great rub and cook it quickly at a high temperature. Don't forget to let the meat rest. Like with steak, it really makes a difference.

Week 10

Green: Chicken Parmesan
with Pasta and Italian Veggies

Our family rating: 9.5
Your family rating: _____

Yellow: Pork & Pineapple Curry with Rice
and Balsamic Nutty Green Beans

Our family rating: 10
Your family rating: _____

Red: Asian Tuna (or Chicken) Wontons
with Corn on the Cob

Our family rating: 9
Your family rating: _____

Blue: Chicken-Mushroom Leek Pie
and Spinach Salad

Our family rating: 9
Your family rating: _____

Red: Apricot-Ginger Lamb
with Couscous and Asparagus

Our family rating: 10
Your family rating: _____

Chicken Parmesan
with Pasta and Italian Veggies

Instructions:

Don't change yet! Take out equipment.
1. Preheat **oven** to **375° F.**
    Place chicken breasts in a large lasagna or cake pan. Sprinkle with Parmesan cheese. Pour pasta sauce evenly over the top.

    Cover with aluminum foil and place in preheated **oven.** Set timer for 35 minutes.

    ...meanwhile...
2. Rinse baby carrots and grape tomatoes. Place in a salad bowl. Rinse, then slice cucumber into chunks, adding to salad bowl as you cut. Rinse, then quarter mushrooms, adding to bowl as you cut. Cut onion into small chunks and add to bowl. Drizzle with dressing and toss to coat. Set aside in **fridge** for dinner or serve as an appetizer.

    ...when timer rings for chicken...
3. Leave chicken in the oven. *The timer was just to remind you it's time to start cooking the pasta. (Chicken cooks for about 55 minutes.)* Fill a large **stove-top** pot with water and bring to a boil for pasta.
    Add pasta to boiling water. Set timer for 11 minutes or follow package directions.

    ...when timer rings for pasta...
    Rinse pasta in a colander under hot water, return to pot and toss with olive oil and basil.

4. Remove chicken from oven and sprinkle cheeses over top. Return to **oven** and reset timer for 5 minutes; bake until cheese is melted.

    Serve chicken on top of pasta or on the side. This is a great dish to get kids involved because it's really easy to assemble the chicken.

Ingredients:

Take out ingredients.

5 chicken breasts, boneless, skinless (1 1/2 lbs or 675 g)
1/4 cup Parmesan cheese, light, grated
1 can pasta sauce (24 oz or 680 mL)
aluminum foil

1 cup baby carrots
1 cup grape tomatoes
1 English cucumber
5 mushrooms
1/8 of a red onion (optional)
2 Tbsp Italian dressing, light

water

3/4 lb or 350 g penne pasta

1 tsp olive oil, extra-virgin
1 tsp basil leaves

1 1/2 cups mozzarella cheese, part-skim, shredded
2 Tbsp Parmesan cheese, light, grated

Serves 4-6

DINNER IS READY IN 60 MINUTES

Equipment List:

Large lasagna or cake pan
Large stove-top pot
Cutting board
Colander
Salad bowl
2 stirring spoons
Sharp veggie knife
Can opener
Measuring cups and spoons
Aluminum foil

Per serving:

Calories	538
Fat	11.1 g
Protein	45.3 g
Carbohydrate	61.6 g
Fiber	3.8 g
Sodium	951 mg

U.S. Food Exchanges:		Cdn. Food Choices:	
3	Starch	3	Carb
5	Meat-very lean	5	Meat/Alt
3	Vegetable	1	Other Carb

Pork & Pineapple Curry with Rice and Balsamic Nutty Green Beans

Instructions:

Don't change yet! Take out equipment.

1. Heat oil in a large nonstick **fry pan** or wok at medium-high.
    Cut onion into large chunks, adding to pan as you cut. Stir until translucent. Cut chops into large cubes (about 8-10 cubes per chop), adding to pan as you cut. Sauté until all sides are browned.

    …meanwhile…

2. Combine rice and water in a large microwave-safe pot. Cover and **microwave** at high 10 minutes, then medium 10 minutes.

3. Add curry and ginger to meat pan and stir.

    Cut peppers into large chunks, adding to pan as you cut. Stir.
    Add mushroom soup and stir to combine.
    Add pineapple with juice, stir to combine and **reduce heat** to a high simmer.

    …meanwhile…

4. Heat oil in a different large nonstick **fry pan** or wok at medium heat. Rinse beans in a colander. Shake off excess water. Add beans to pan. Splash on balsamic vinegar and sprinkle with nuts.

    …when timer rings for rice…

5. Remove rice from microwave, lift with fork, return lid and let rest a few minutes.

    *Beans are ready when they are glazed and tender, but crunchy. Use an instant-read thermometer to make sure the internal temp of your largest piece of pork is **170° F**.*

    This will become a family favorite!

Ingredients:

Take out ingredients.
1 tsp olive oil, extra-virgin

1/4 of a red onion
3 thick pork loin chops, boneless, trimmed (1 lb or 450 g)

1 1/2 cups basmati or white rice
3 cups water

1 Tbsp curry powder
1 tsp fresh ginger (from a jar)
1/2 of a red pepper
1/2 of a green pepper
1 can cream of mushroom soup, reduced-sodium (10 oz or 284 mL)
1 can pineapple chunks with liquid (14 oz or 398 mL)

1 tsp olive oil, extra-virgin
4 cups frozen green beans

1 Tbsp balsamic vinegar
2 Tbsp peanuts or slivered almonds, unsalted

<u>**Serves 4-6**</u>

30 MINUTES   READY, *LET'S EAT!*

Equipment List:

2 large nonstick fry pans
  (or woks)
Large microwave-safe pot w/lid
2 cutting boards
Colander
Flipper
Instant-read thermometer
Sharp meat knife
Sharp veggie knife
Stirring spoon
Can opener
Fork
Measuring cups and spoons

Per serving:

Calories	386
Fat	6.4 g
Protein	23.4 g
Carbohydrate	59.8 g
Fiber	5.2 g
Sodium	344 mg

U.S. Food Exchanges:		Cdn. Food Choices:	
2	Starch	2 1/2	Carb
3	Meat-lean	3	Meat/Alt
1	Fruit	1	Other Carb
1	Vegetable		

Asian Tuna (or Chicken) Wontons with Corn on the Cob

Instructions:

Don't change yet! Take out equipment.
1. Preheat **oven** to **350° F**.

2. Whisk together garlic, sesame oil, Sambal Oelek, Kepac Manis, lime juice and honey in a large mixing bowl.

Drain water from tuna or chicken. Crumble into dressing. Crush peanuts (or buy them that way) and add to bowl. Add coleslaw mix and toss to coat. Set aside, but toss again later, just before serving.

...meanwhile...
3. Brush the inside of 2 muffin tins thoroughly with peanut oil (to make 24). Place a wonton wrapper in each cup. Brush any dry spots you see on the tops, especially the tips. Place in preheated **oven**. Set timer for 6-7 minutes or bake until golden brown.

4. Wrap husked corn in foil. Place on lower rack of preheated **oven**.

...when timer rings for wonton cups...
5. Remove cups from **oven** and let cool on rack. Leave corn in and reset timer for 5 minutes.

Serve the wonton cups and filling at the table. Fill as you go so the wonton cups stay crunchy. You can add toppings such as sprouts, red pepper and cilantro. Serve beside hot corn, with butter...if you must.

This is a modern-day salad/sandwich with corn on the cob. It's sophisticated for the parents yet fun for the kids. You'll love the fresh taste and I warn you, it's addictive.

Ingredients:

Take out ingredients.

Dressing
1 1/2 tsp fresh garlic (from a jar)
1/2 tsp sesame oil
1/2 tsp Sambal Oelek (crushed chili paste)
   (add more if you like it hot)
1/4 cup Kepac Manis, sweet soy sauce
   (or use mushroom soy and honey)
3 Tbsp lime juice, bottled
1 Tbsp liquid honey

2 cans solid tuna in water, drained
   (6 1/2 oz or 180 g each) or use chicken
3 Tbsp crushed peanuts, unsalted
4 cups coleslaw mix
   I like the colorful one with carrots.

1 Tbsp peanut oil
24 wonton wrappers (3 1/2" square)
You can skip this step and wrap the filling in warm tortillas or use taco shells, but we think wontons really make a difference.

4-6 ears of corn (can use frozen)
aluminum foil

fresh bean sprouts (optional)
red bell pepper (optional)
cilantro (optional)
butter (optional for corn)

Any leftovers are perfect for lunch the next day. Make sure you keep the cups and filling separate.

Serves 6

30 MINUTES   READY, *LET'S EAT!*

Equipment List:

2 muffin tins
Cooling rack
Large mixing bowl
Whisk
Large serving spoon
Pastry brush
Can opener
Measuring cups and spoons
Aluminum foil

Per serving:

Calories	341
Fat	7.4 g
Protein	21.3 g
Carbohydrate	49.8 g
Fiber	3.4 g
Sodium	586 mg

U.S. Food Exchanges:		Cdn. Food Choices:	
2	Starch	2	Carb
2	Meat-very lean	2	Meat/Alt
1	Fat	1/2	Fat
1	Other Carb	1	Other Carb

15 to prep

Chicken-Mushroom Leek Pie and Spinach Salad

Instructions:

...the night before...
Take out equipment.

1. Cut the rough parts off each end of the leeks. Slice the leeks in half lengthwise. Pull the leeks apart and rinse each piece thoroughly under water in a colander. This is extremely important, unless you like crunching on sand! Place leeks in a large plastic bag or container and store in **fridge**.

   ...when you get home...

2. Preheat **oven** to 375° F. Heat oil in a large **stove-top** pot at medium. Cut chicken into bite-size pieces, adding to pot as you cut. Slice leeks into slivers, adding to pot as you slice. Stir. Rinse, then slice celery, adding to pot as you cut. Cut mushrooms into quarters and add to pot. Add spices and garlic. Stir and **remove from heat**. Let stand to cool slightly.

3. Spray a deep-dish pie plate (preferably glass) with cooking spray. Lay sheets of phyllo across the sprayed pie plate in every direction so that the phyllo drapes over the entire edge of pie plate. *They will overlap.* Melt butter for 10 seconds in **microwave**, then stir in olive oil. Set aside.
   Stir crumbled feta and Parmesan into the leek and chicken pot. Add one egg at a time, stirring to combine. Scoop the leek and chicken filling into the pie plate.

   Bring each layer of phyllo over the filling, brushing butter mixture between layers as you go. Brush any leftover butter on top. Sprinkle with a little parsley and cover with a foil tent. Place in preheated **oven**. Set timer for 50 minutes.

   ...meanwhile...

4. Rinse spinach in basket of salad spinner and spin dry. Set out croutons and salad dressing. *Set aside or eat as an appetizer while pie is cooking.*

Ingredients:

Take out ingredients.
2 leeks

1 tsp olive oil, extra-virgin
3 chicken breasts, boneless, skinless (1 lb or 450 g)
reserved leeks
4 ribs celery
10 mushrooms
1/2 tsp ground pepper
pinch salt
1/2 tsp Mrs. Dash Original seasoning
1 1/2 Tbsp dried dill (or 1/2 cup fresh)
2 tsp fresh garlic (from a jar)

cooking spray
4 sheets phyllo pastry

1 tsp butter
2 tsp olive oil, extra-virgin

10 oz or 300 g feta cheese, light
1/4 cup Parmesan cheese, light, grated
2 eggs

1 tsp parsley flakes
aluminum foil

1 bag spinach leaves (12 oz or 350 g)
3/4 cup croutons
1/3 cup favorite salad dressing, fat-free
<u>Serves 6-8</u>

60 MINUTES   READY, *LET'S EAT!*

Equipment List:

…the night before…
Colander & Cutting board
Sharp veggie knife
Large plastic bag or container
…when you get home…
Large stove-top pot
2 cutting boards
Deep-dish pie plate, glass is best
Small microwave-safe bowl
Salad spinner & Salad bowl
Salad tongs & Pastry brush
Colander & 2 stirring spoons
Sharp meat & veggie knives
Large serving spoon
Measuring cups and spoons
Aluminum foil

Per serving:

Calories	287
Fat	12.6 g
Protein	27.9 g
Carbohydrate	17.1 g
Fiber	2.5 g
Sodium	751 mg

U.S. Food Exchanges:		Cdn. Food Choices:	
1	Starch	1	Carb
3 1/2	Meat-lean	3 1/2	Meat/Alt
1/2	Fat	1/2	Fat

Apricot-Ginger Lamb, with Couscous and Asparagus

Instructions:

Don't change yet! Take out equipment.

1. Preheat **oven** to **425° F**.
   Spray an oven-safe casserole or cake pan with cooking spray. Place lamb in casserole (bone side down) and drizzle with olive oil.

   Combine garlic, ginger, thyme and jam in a small mixing bowl. Spread mixture evenly over top of lamb.

   Drizzle lamb with lime juice.
   Place in preheated **oven**. Set timer for 25 minutes.

2. Add water and chicken broth to a small **stove-top** pot and bring to a boil.
   Add couscous to pot and stir.
   Remove from heat.
   Chop tomato and add to pot.
   Add salsa and stir.
   Chop and add cilantro if you wish.
   Cover and let stand 5 minutes.

   ...when timer rings for lamb...

3. Remove lamb from oven and cover tightly with foil.
   Let it rest while asparagus is cooking.

   ...meanwhile...

4. Snap off bottom nodes of asparagus and discard. Rinse in colander or steamer basket. Place a small amount of water in the bottom of a **stove-top** pot and bring to a full boil with the asparagus in the basket above. Cover and set timer for 4 minutes...or microwave for the same amount of time. *See page 34.*
   ...when timer rings for asparagus...
   Drain water. Toss in pot with butter and salt.

   Cut lamb into individual ribs before serving.

Ingredients:

Take out ingredients.

cooking spray
2 racks of lamb (approx 16 ribs), trimmed (1 1/2 lbs or 675 g)
2 tsp olive oil, extra-virgin

2 Tbsp fresh garlic (from a jar)
1 Tbsp fresh ginger (from a jar)
1 1/2 tsp dried thyme leaves
1/3 cup apricot jam

1-2 Tbsp lime juice

3/4 cup water
1 can chicken broth, reduced-sodium (10 oz or 284 mL)
1 cup whole-wheat couscous
1 Roma tomato
2 Tbsp salsa
cilantro (optional)

heavy aluminum foil

20 asparagus spears (1 lb or 450 g)

water

1 tsp butter (optional)
pinch of salt (optional)

<u>Serves 4</u>

30 MINUTES   READY, *LET'S EAT!*

Equipment List:

Oven-safe casserole or cake pan
Small stove-top pot w/lid
Stove-top pot w/steamer basket
2 cutting boards
Small mixing bowl
Stirring spoon
Sharp veggie knife
Sharp meat knife
Can opener
Measuring cups and spoons
Aluminum foil

Per serving:

Calories	401
Fat	9.4 g
Protein	23.5 g
Carbohydrate	57.8 g
Fiber	8.3 g
Sodium	268 mg

U.S. Food Exchanges:		Cdn. Food Choices:	
3	Starch	3	Carb
2	Meat-lean	2	Meat/Alt
1	Fat	1	Fat
1/2	Other Carb	1/2	Other Carb

15
to
prep

GROCERY LISTS

MEATS

Pork top loin roast, boneless, trimmed
  (3 lbs or 1350 g)
Chicken breasts, boneless, skinless
  (1 1/3 lbs or 600 g)
Chicken thighs (10-12) boneless, skinless
  (1 1/2 lbs or 675 g)
Ground beef, extra-lean (1 lb or 450 g)

DAIRY

Butter
Cream, 10% milk fat (1/4 cup)
Milk, 1% milk fat
Cheddar cheese, light, shredded (2 cups)
Parmesan cheese, light, grated (optional for Pasta)

PRODUCE

Fresh garlic (from a jar)
Fresh ginger (from a jar)
Onion, sweet white, large (1)
Onion (1)
Potatoes (3 large)
Baby potatoes (20) or 4 large thin-skinned potatoes
Chives (optional for Cheddar Soup)
Green leaf lettuce (1 head)
Cilantro (optional for Couscous)
Veggies (1 cup): tomato, pepper, broccoli, carrot...
Asparagus spears (20)
Broccoli florets (1 lb or 450 g)
Zucchini, small (1)
Mushrooms (8)

DRY ESSENTIALS

Bow tie pasta (3 cups)
Basmati rice (1 1/2 cups)
Couscous, whole-wheat (1 1/2 cups)
Croutons (optional for Salad)

BAKERY

Whole-wheat dinner rolls, small (6)

SPICES

Chili powder
Cinnamon
Cumin, ground
Garlic & herb seasoning, salt-free
Garlic powder
Mrs. Dash Original seasoning
Onion flakes
Parsley flakes
Rosemary leaves
Turmeric
Salt & Pepper

BAKING GOODS

Cooking spray
Canola oil
Olive oil, extra-virgin
Sesame oil
Brown sugar
Flour
Dry brown gravy mix (I like Bisto)
Pine nuts (1/2 cup) (can use matchstick almonds)
Craisins (can use raisins)

HELPERS

1 can pasta sauce (24 oz or 680 mL) (I like spicy)
Beef broth, reduced-sodium (1 cup)
Chicken broth, reduced-sodium (3 1/2 cups)
Vegetable bouillon powder
Sweet Thai chili sauce
Chunky salsa (1 3/4 cups)
Vinaigrette salad dressing, light, your favorite
Lime juice
Applesauce, unsweetened, single-serve container
Liquid honey

FROZEN FOODS

Baby peas (2 cups)
Corn (2 cups)

OTHER

Aluminum foil

Custom Grocery List

RECIPE NAME   Page

_____

_____

_____

_____

_____

MEATS

DAIRY

PRODUCE

DRY ESSENTIALS

SPICES

BAKING GOODS

HELPERS

FROZEN FOODS

BAKERY

OTHER

MEATS

Ground beef, lean (2 lbs or 900 g)
Bacon strips, precooked (8) (optional for Burgers)
Bacon bits (optional for Spinach Salad)
Chicken breasts, boneless, skinless (8)
  (approx 3 lbs or 1.3 kg) for 2 meals
Top sirloin or tenderloin steak, boneless, trimmed,
  2 inches thick (1 1/2 lbs or 675 g)

DAIRY

Cheddar cheese, light, shredded (1/2 cup)
Feta cheese, light, crumbled (1/3 cup)
Ricotta cheese (1 cup)
Parmesan cheese, light, grated (1/2 cup) for 2 meals
Mozzarella cheese, part-skim, shredded (1/2 cup)
Cottage cheese, 1% (1/2 cup)
Egg (1)
Butter
Milk, 1% milk fat
Udon noodles, 2 pkgs (7 oz or 200 g each) (thick
  Japanese wheat noodles, usually fresh in deli or
  dairy section, can replace with Shanghai noodles)

PRODUCE

Fresh garlic (from a jar) & Fresh ginger (from a jar)
Onion (1) & Green onions (10) for 2 meals
Shallot (1)
Baby carrots (4 cups) & Celery rib (1)
Veggies (4 cups): baby carrots, snap peas, broccoli
Asparagus (1 lb or 450 g)
Zucchini, small (1) (can use English cucumber)
Red bell pepper (2) & Green bell pepper (1)
Tomatoes (2)
Lettuce (optional for Burgers)
Baby spinach, 1 bag (8 oz or 225 g)
Romaine lettuce, 1 bag (12 oz or 350 g)
Brown mushrooms (12)
Dry shitake mushrooms (1/2 cup) (or use fresh
  enoki mushrooms, or 1 1/2 cups white or brown)
Apple or mango (1) (optional for Crunchy Salad)

BAKERY

Multigrain hamburger buns (8)

SPICES

Chili powder & Dry mustard
Garlic powder & Ginger powder
Italian seasoning, salt-free
Seasoning salt (optional for Fries)
Pepper

BAKING GOODS

Canola oil & Olive oil, extra-virgin
Cooking spray (olive oil variety)
Cider vinegar
Flour & Dark brown sugar
Dry brown gravy mix (I like Bisto)
Nuts, your choice, almonds, peanuts…

HELPERS

1 can cream of mushroom soup (10 oz or 284 mL)
Chicken broth, reduced-sodium (60 oz or 1.8 L)
1 can tomato-basil pasta sauce (24 oz or 680 mL)
1 can stewed tomatoes (14 oz or 398 mL)
Tabasco sauce & Worcestershire sauce
Soy sauce, reduced-sodium
Horseradish (optional for Burgers)
Mayonnaise, light
Ketchup
Ranch dressing, fat-free
Caesar salad dressing, light
Salad dressing, your favorite (I like ginger-wasabi)
Miso paste (1/4 cup) (also named Japanese soybean
  paste; in Asian foods, can replace with 1 1/2 Tbsp
  yeast extract spread & 2 Tbsp peanut butter)
1 can pineapple chunks (14 oz or 398 mL)

FROZEN FOODS

Chopped spinach (3 1/2 oz or 100 g)
Crinkle-cut French fries (1 lb or 450 g)

OTHER

Red wine (1/4 cup) (can use nonalcoholic)
Squirt bottle (found at home improvement store)
Aluminum foil

DRY ESSENTIALS

Croutons (optional for Spinach Salad)
Manicotti pasta shells, 24 large (8 oz or 225 g)
  (also named conchiglioni rigati)
Chow mein egg noodles (1 cup)
Basmati or white rice (1 1/2 cups)

Custom Grocery List

RECIPE NAME   Page

_____

_____

_____

_____

_____

MEATS

DAIRY

PRODUCE

DRY ESSENTIALS

SPICES

BAKING GOODS

HELPERS

FROZEN FOODS

BAKERY

OTHER

RECIPE NAME	Page

MEATS

Roaster chicken, deli cooked (3 cups cut chicken)
Lean pork ribs, back or side (2 1/2 lbs or 1125 g)
  (can double amount to have extra)
Chicken thighs with skin (10) (2 lbs or 900 g)
Ground beef, extra-lean (1 1/2 lbs or 675 g)
Salmon fillets, boneless, skinless (1 1/2 lbs or 675 g)

DAIRY

Butter
Milk, 1% milk fat (1/4 cup)

PRODUCE

Onions (2)
Red onion (1)
Green onions (2)
Potatoes, 4 large (2 lbs or 900 g)
Tomatoes, Roma (2)
Mushrooms, small (15), for 2 meals
Red bell peppers (2) for 2 meals
Green bell pepper (1)
Zucchini, small (1)
English cucumber (1) or broccoli
Broccoli florets (1 lb or 450 g)
Asparagus spears (20)
Spinach, 1 bag (12 oz or 350 g)
Romaine lettuce, 1/2 bag (6 oz or 175 g)
Cilantro
Cantaloupe (1)

DRY ESSENTIALS

Couscous (1 cup)
Basmati or white rice (1 1/2 cups)
Round rice papers (optional for Peking Chicken)
  (found in the ethnic section of your grocer)

OTHER

Waxed paper

SPICES

Curry powder
Chipotle seasoning
Dill, dried
Garlic & herb seasoning, salt-free
Mrs. Dash Table Blend seasoning
Onion flakes
Parsley flakes
Poultry seasoning
Salt

BAKING GOODS

Cooking spray
Cornstarch
Flour
Dry brown gravy mix (I like Bisto)
Cashews, unsalted (optional for Spinach Salad)
Pine nuts (1/2 cup)
Coconut, shredded, unsweetened

HELPERS

1 can consommé soup (10 oz or 284 mL)
1 can beef broth, reduced-sodium
  (10 oz or 284 mL)
Chicken broth, reduced-sodium (2 Tbsp)
  (or use wine or water)
1 can Italian stewed tomatoes (19 oz or 540 mL)
Cranberry sauce, whole-berry (1/2 cup)
Honey-garlic sauce, 2 jars (12 oz or 341 mL each)
  for 2 meals (I like VH brand)
Plum sauce (I like VH brand)
Hoisin sauce
Basil pesto
Salad dressing, fat-free, your favorite

FROZEN FOODS

Corn (1 cup) (I like Peaches & Cream variety)

BAKERY

Multigrain bread, 1 loaf sliced (18 slices)
Bread rolls (6) (optional for Honey-Garlic Ribs)

Custom Grocery List

RECIPE NAME   Page

_____

_____

_____

_____

_____

MEATS

DAIRY

PRODUCE

DRY ESSENTIALS

SPICES

BAKING GOODS

HELPERS

FROZEN FOODS

BAKERY

OTHER

MEATS

Chicken thighs, boneless, skinless (10-12)
   (1 3/4 lbs or 800 g)
Lamb chops, bone-in, trimmed (2 lbs or 900 g)
   (or use pork chops)
Ground chicken, lean (3/4 lb or 350 g)
Ground turkey, lean (3/4 lb or 350 g)
Cajun or shaved honey ham, lean, cooked
   (2 oz or 57 g)
Shrimp, large, cooked, peeled and deveined
   (1 lb or 450 g) (or use chicken breast)

DAIRY

Butter & Egg (1)
Milk, 1% milk fat
Parmesan cheese, grated, light (1 cup) for 2 meals
Feta cheese, light, crumbled (1/2 cup)
Mozzarella cheese, part-skim, shredded (1/2 cup)
Swiss cheese, light, thin slices (2 oz or 57 g)
Pillsbury pizza crust (1) in a tube (10 oz or 283 g)

PRODUCE

Fresh garlic (from a jar) & Fresh ginger (from a jar)
Onion, large (1)
Sweet red onion (1)
Green onions (2)
Broccoli florets (1 lb or 450 g)
Tomato & Lettuce (optional for Burgers)
Eggplant or zucchini, slices (1 cup)
Asparagus spears (26) for 2 meals
Coleslaw mix, 4 cups (8 oz or 225 g)
   (I like the colorful one with carrots)
Baby spinach, 1 bag (12 oz or 350 g)
Macintosh or Spartan apple (1)
Mandarin oranges (3)

DRY ESSENTIALS

Linguini pasta (12 oz or 375 g)
Steam-fried egg noodles (1 cup)
Basmati rice (3 cups) for 2 meals
Cornflake crumbs (1/2 cup)

FROZEN FOODS

Peas (4 cups)

SPICES

Cinnamon stick (1)
Cloves, whole (4-5) (optional for Basmati Rice)
Curry powder
Garam masala (Indian spice blend)
Garlic & herb seasoning blend, salt-free
Ginger powder
Grill spice blend, salt-free
Hot chili flakes
Italian seasoning
Mustard powder
Onion flakes (1/4 cup)
Onion powder
Smoked paprika (or use paprika and Liquid Smoke)
Salt & Pepper

BAKING GOODS

Cooking spray
Canola oil
Olive oil, extra-virgin
Sesame oil
Vinegar & Rice vinegar
Flour
Sugar & Brown sugar
Cashews, unsalted (1/2 cup)
Pecan pieces (can use pecans and matchstick
   almonds)
Dried apricots (2-3) (can buy these in bulk section)
Craisins (1/4 cup)

HELPERS

1 can beef broth, reduced-sodium
   (10 oz or 284 mL)
1 can tomatoes, diced (14 oz or 398 mL)
Basil pesto (1/4 cup)
Soy sauce, reduced-sodium
Salad dressing, fat-free, your favorite
Mayonnaise, light
Hot pepper jelly (jalapeño or red pepper jelly)
   (optional for Cordon Bleu Burgers)
Peanut butter, light

BAKERY

Naan bread pieces (4-6) (optional for Lamb Masala)
Hamburger buns, multigrain (6)

OTHER

White wine (1/2 cup)

Custom Grocery List

RECIPE NAME   Page

_____

_____

_____

_____

_____

MEATS

DAIRY

PRODUCE

DRY ESSENTIALS

SPICES

BAKING GOODS

HELPERS

FROZEN FOODS

BAKERY

OTHER

MEATS

Chicken breasts, boneless, skinless (4)
  (1 1/2 lbs or 675 g)
Chicken thighs, boneless, skinless (10-12)
  (1 3/4 lbs or 800 g)
Top sirloin or tenderloin steak, boneless, trimmed
  2 inches thick (1 1/2 lbs or 675 g)
Shrimp, large, cooked, deveined with tails
  (1 lb or 450 g), 1 cup more if using in Quiche
Bacon bits (optional for Caesar Salad)

DAIRY

Butter
Eggs, large (4)
Cream, 10% milk fat (1/4 cup)
Milk, 1% milk fat
Sour cream, no-fat (1/4 cup)
Gruyère cheese (1/4 cup)
Mozzarella cheese, part-skim (1/4 cup)
Cheddar cheese, light (1/2 cup) (can use old)
Aged cheddar cheese, light, shredded (1/2 cup)
Feta cheese, light, (1/4 cup) (can use cheddar)
Parmesan cheese, light, grated

PRODUCE

Gourmet Caesar salad dressing, lower-fat
Fresh garlic (from a jar) & Fresh ginger (from a jar)
Baker potatoes, 2 large (1 lb or 225 g)
Onion (1)
Sweet red onion (1)
Green onion (1), more if using on Stuffed Potatoes
Cilantro (optional for Thai Shrimp)
Baby spinach, 1 bag (12 oz or 350 g)
Romaine lettuce, large head (1)
Lemongrass (from a tube or use fresh)
Mushrooms (4)
Red bell pepper (1)
Zucchini (optional for Quiche)
Tomato, Roma (optional for Quiche)
Grape tomatoes (8-12) (optional for Thai Shrimp)
Broccoli florets (1 1/2 lbs or 675 g) for 3 meals
Bok choy (1/2 lb or 225 g) (or use broccoli florets)
Mandarin oranges (2) (optional for Thai Shrimp)

SPICES

Basil leaves
Chinese five spice powder
Lemon pepper
Mrs. Dash Original seasoning
Paprika
Parsley flakes
Salt & Pepper

BAKING GOODS

Cooking spray
Olive oil, extra-virgin
Sesame oil
Brown sugar
Biscuit mix (1/2 cup) (I like Bisquick brand)
Matchstick almonds (1 cup)
Pecan pieces (1 cup)
Cashews (optional for Thai Shrimp)

HELPERS

1 can chicken broth, reduced-sodium
  (10 oz or 284 mL)
Fruit vinaigrette salad dressing, light, your favorite
Mayonnaise, no-fat
Ketchup & BBQ sauce
Soy sauce, reduced-sodium
Sweet Thai chili sauce (1/2 cup)
Fish sauce
Lime juice
Mandarin oranges, single-serve size
Liquid honey
Peanut butter, light

FROZEN FOODS

Bean-carrot mix (4 cups) (can use green beans)
Wild blueberries (1 cup)

DRY ESSENTIALS

Croutons
Basmati or white rice (1 1/2 cups)
Cavatappi pasta, 4 cups (10 oz or 283 g)
  (can use any spiral pasta)
Rice noodles (10 oz or 284 g)

OTHER

Toothpicks
Aluminum foil
Dry white wine (1/2 cup) (can be nonalcoholic)

Custom Grocery List

RECIPE NAME   Page

_____

_____

_____

_____

_____

MEATS

DAIRY

PRODUCE

DRY ESSENTIALS

SPICES

BAKING GOODS

HELPERS

FROZEN FOODS

BAKERY

OTHER

MEATS

Flank steak, trimmed (1 1/2 lbs or 675 g)
Top sirloin steak, boneless, trimmed, very thick
  (1 1/2 lbs or 675 g)
Smoked turkey sausages, fully cooked (3)
  (similar to pepperoni sticks)
Chicken breasts, boneless, skinless (3)
  (1 lb or 450 g)
Shrimp, large, cooked, deveined, tail on (1 lb or 450 g)

DAIRY

Butter
Milk, 1% milk fat
Cream, 10% milk fat (1/2 cup)
Vanilla yogurt, light (1 cup)
Parmesan cheese, light, grated
Mozzarella cheese, part-skim, shredded (1/2 cup)
  (or use cheddar cheese)
Cheddar cheese, light, shredded (1/4 cup)
Feta cheese, light (1/4 cup)

PRODUCE

Garlic cloves (8)
Fresh garlic (from a jar) & Fresh ginger (from a jar)
Red onion (2) for 2 meals
Green onions (3 + 1 bunch)
Vine tomatoes, firm, medium (9) for 2 meals
  (can use 12 Roma tomatoes)
Mushrooms (6)
Carrot (1) & Celery ribs (2)
Broccoli florets (1 lb or 450 g)
Corn on the cob (4-6)
Mixed salad greens, 1 bag (12 oz or 350 g)
Baby spinach, 1 bag (12 oz or 350 g)
Green salad, 1 bag (8 oz or 225 g) (optional for
  Strawberry Skewers)
Strawberries (28) for 2 meals
Blackberries (optional for Mixed Salad Greens)

BAKERY

12" pizza crust (you want a nice soft white crust)

DRY ESSENTIALS

Basmati rice (3 cups) for 2 meals

SPICES

Basil leaves
Bay leaves, dried or fresh
Cayenne pepper
Cinnamon
Curry powder
Parsley flakes
Mrs. Dash Original seasoning
Oregano
Peppercorns, mixed
Salt & Pepper

BAKING GOODS

Canola oil
Olive oil, extra-virgin
Rice vinegar
Red wine vinegar
Sugar
Flour
Dry gravy mix for chicken (I like Bisto)
Cashews, unsalted (1/2 cup)
Nuts (optional for Mixed Salad Greens)

HELPERS

1 can red pepper stewed tomatoes
  (19 oz or 540 mL)
Chicken broth, reduced-sodium, for 2 meals
  (30 oz or 900 mL)
Soy sauce, reduced-sodium
Hoisin sauce
Fish sauce
Sweet Thai chili sauce
Sambal Oelek (crushed chili paste)
  (optional for Hoisin Beef)
Salad dressing, no-fat, your favorite
  (I like creamy Vidalia onion)

FROZEN FOODS

Green beans (1 lb or 450 g)
Okra, 1 pkg cut (10 oz or 300 g)
Mixed bell peppers (1 cup)
Puff pastry (7 oz or 200 g)

OTHER

Red wine (1 Tbsp)
Brandy (1 Tbsp) or use apple jelly
Aluminum foil
Skewers (4)

Custom Grocery List

RECIPE NAME   Page

_____

_____

_____

_____

_____

MEATS

DAIRY

PRODUCE

DRY ESSENTIALS

SPICES

BAKING GOODS

HELPERS

FROZEN FOODS

BAKERY

OTHER

MEATS

Flank steak, trimmed (1 1/2 lbs or 675 g)
Chicken breasts, large, boneless, skinless (4)
  (1 1/2 lbs or 675 g)
Chicken wings (12-16) (1 1/2 lbs or 675 g)
Lean cooked ham, 6 thin slices (2 oz or 60 g)
Bacon slices (4)

DAIRY

Butter
Milk, 1% milk fat
Cream, 10% milk fat (1/2 cup)
Feta cheese, light (optional for Green Salad)
Parmesan cheese, light, grated
Gruyère cheese, shredded (1/2 cup)
Tex-Mex cheese, shredded (1/4 cup)
Swiss cheese, light, 6 thin slices (2 oz or 60 g)

PRODUCE

Fresh garlic (from a jar)
Onion (2) for 2 meals
Red onion (1)
Baby potatoes (20) or 4 large potatoes
Red bell pepper (1) & Green bell pepper (1)
Orange or yellow bell pepper (1)
Mushrooms (6)
Portabella mushrooms, large (4)
Zucchini, small (1)
Asparagus spears (20)
Broccoli florets (1 lb or 450 g)
Mixed salad greens, 1 bag (12 oz or 350 g)
Cilantro (optional for Stir-Fry)
Pineapple slices (4) (can be canned)
Strawberries (5)

DRY ESSENTIALS

Basmati rice (1 1/2 cups)
Penne pasta (4 cups)
Dry white navy beans (1 1/4 cup)
Stoned wheat crackers, reduced-sodium, crumbled
  (approx 30 small crackers)

BAKERY

Multigrain bread (1 loaf)

SPICES

Basil leaves (optional for Pasta)
Chili powder
Cumin, ground
Garlic & herb seasoning, salt-free
Mrs. Dash Original seasoning
Paprika
Pepper

BAKING GOODS

Cooking spray
Olive oil, extra-virgin
Vinegar
Balsamic vinegar
Flour
Brown sugar
Molasses
Maple syrup
Pine nuts
Nuts (optional for Green Salad)

HELPERS

1 can chicken broth, reduced-sodium
  (10 oz or 284 mL)
1 can Italian diced tomatoes (14 oz or 398 mL)
1 can solid tuna or chicken in water
  (6 1/2 oz or 184 g)
Sun-dried tomatoes (from a jar)
Ketchup, for 2 meals (or banana ketchup for 1)
Dijon mustard
Sambal Oelek (crushed chili paste)
Sweet Thai chili sauce (1/4 cup)
Chunky salsa (1/2 cup)
Strong garlic spare-rib sauce (1 cup)
  (I like VH brand) (or honey-garlic or teriyaki)
Soy sauce, reduced-sodium
Salad dressing, poppy seed, light, or favorite

FROZEN FOODS

Carrot and bean blend (1 lb or 450 g)
Baby peas (1 cup)

OTHER

White wine (1/2 cup)
Toothpicks
Waxed paper
Aluminum foil
Foil grill pan (optional for Chicken Wings)

Custom Grocery List

RECIPE NAME   Page

_____

_____

_____

_____

_____

MEATS

DAIRY

PRODUCE

DRY ESSENTIALS

SPICES

BAKING GOODS

HELPERS

FROZEN FOODS

BAKERY

OTHER

MEATS

Roaster chicken, cooked from deli (2 cups)
Chicken thighs, boneless, skinless (8 large)
  (1 3/4 lbs or 800 g)
Top sirloin or tenderloin steak, boneless, trimmed,
  2 inches thick (1 1/2 lbs or 675 g)
Bacon slices, fully cooked (4)
Salmon fillets, skinless, boneless (4-6 equal parts)
  (1 1/2 lbs or 675 g)

DAIRY

Butter
Milk, 1% milk fat
Feta cheese, light (optional for BLT Salad)
Parmesan cheese, grated, light
Cambozola cheese (1/4 cup) (can use Gorgonzola
  or grated Gruyère)

PRODUCE

Fresh garlic (from a jar) & Fresh ginger (from a jar)
Shallot (1) & Onions, large (2)
Mushrooms (10)
Red bell pepper (1) & Yellow bell pepper (1)
Zucchini, medium (2)
Snap peas (1 lb or 450 g)
Celery ribs (2-3)
Carrots (2-3)
Tomato, hothouse or Roma, firm (1)
Broccoli florets (1 lb or 450 g)
Sweet potato fries (4-6 cups) (found near bagged
  salads) (can use regular fries)
Romaine lettuce, 1 bag (8 oz or 225 g)
Cilantro (optional for Sesame Snap Chicken)

DRY ESSENTIALS

Sesame snaps (8 wafers)
  (sesame-honey crisps found in candy aisle)
Spaghetti pasta, or steam-fried (3/4 lb or 350 g)
Fusilli pasta (2 cups)

BAKERY

French loaves (2) for 2 meals
  (or 1 French loaf and 1 baguette)
Bread crumbs, fine

SPICES

Cayenne
Chipotle seasoning, salt-free
Curry powder
Garlic powder & Ginger powder
Italian seasoning, salt-free
Lemon pepper
Mrs. Dash Original seasoning
Paprika & Parsley flakes
Peppercorn blend or steak spice, salt-free
Salt & Pepper

BAKING GOODS

Cooking spray
Canola oil & Sesame oil
Olive oil, extra-virgin
Flour
Crushed pecans, or crush your own
Cashews, unsalted (optional for Snap Peas)

HELPERS

Vegetable broth, reduced-sodium (3 1/2-4 cups)
Chicken broth, reduced-sodium (2 cups)
1 can beef broth, reduced-sodium
  (10 oz or 284 mL)
1 can mixed beans (19 oz or 540 mL)
  (kidney, garbanzo, combinations vary)
1 can tomatoes, diced (14 oz or 398 mL)
Tomato paste (2 Tbsp)
Basil pesto (from a jar)
Mayonnaise, light
Sweet green relish
Hot pepper relish (optional for Tartar Sauce)
Worcestershire sauce
Soy sauce, reduced-sodium
Ranch or blue cheese dressing, light, or favorite
Lemon juice
Berry jam (three-fruit blend)
Liquid honey

FROZEN FOODS

Peas (1 cup)
Puff pastry patty shells, 1 pkg of 6 (10 oz or 300 g)
  (I like Tenderflake)

OTHER

White wine (1 cup)
Waxed paper

Custom Grocery List

RECIPE NAME   Page

_____

_____

_____

_____

_____

MEATS

DAIRY

PRODUCE

DRY ESSENTIALS

SPICES

BAKING GOODS

HELPERS

FROZEN FOODS

BAKERY

OTHER

RECIPE NAME	Page
Chicken & Sun-Dried Tomato Pasta, Broccoli	138
Taco Pizza, Melon Salad	140
Sesame-Crusted Salmon, Potatoes, Fruit	142
Canadian Maple Turkey Chili, Fresh Veggies	144
Apple-Cin Pork Chops, Rice Stuffing, Carrots	146

MEATS

Ground turkey (1 lb or 450 g)
Chicken breasts, boneless, skinless (3) (1 lb or 450 g)
Ground beef, extra-lean (1/2 lb or 225 g)
Pork loin chops, boneless, trimmed, thick (6)
  (2 lbs or 900 g)
Bacon, fully cooked (10 slices) for 2 meals
Salmon fillets, boneless, skinless (6)
  (1 1/2 lbs or 675 g)

DAIRY

Butter
Milk, 1% milk fat
Sour cream, reduced-fat
French vanilla yogurt (optional for dipping Fruit)
Mozzarella cheese, part-skim, shredded (1 cup)

PRODUCE

Fresh garlic (from a jar)
Potatoes, large, thin-skinned (4-6) (2 lbs or 900 g)
Red onion (1) & Onion (3) for 3 meals
Green onions (2)
Baby carrots (4 cups) & Celery ribs, large (4)
Mushrooms (22) for 3 meals
Green bell pepper (1) & Red bell pepper (1)
Tomato, large (1) & Tomatoes, Roma (2)
Broccoli florets (1 lb or 450 g)
Raw veggies, broccoli & cauliflower (1 pkg)
  (1 lb or 450 g) (or cut your own)
Green leaf lettuce (1 head)
Cilantro
Grapefruit (2-3) (can use large oranges)
Cantaloupe (1) & Melon of choice, small (1)
Strawberries (8) & Red grapes, seedless (2 cups)
Spartan or Macintosh apples, large (2-3)

DRY ESSENTIALS

Spaghetti pasta (12 oz or 350 g)
White & wild rice blend (I like Canoe brand)
Croutons

OTHER

Paper towels
White wine (1/4 cup), can be nonalcoholic

SPICES

Basil leaves
Cayenne (optional for Chili)
Chili powder & Cinnamon
Cumin, ground, & Garlic powder
Hot chili flakes
Marjoram (can use basil)
Parsley flakes & Oregano leaves
Onion flakes & Poultry seasoning
Sesame seeds, toasted (1/2 cup)
Turmeric
Salt & Pepper

BAKING GOODS

Cooking spray
Cooking spray, olive oil variety
Canola oil & Olive oil, extra-virgin
Brown sugar
Maple syrup
Craisins (can use raisins)

HELPERS

Chicken broth, reduced-sodium (2 cups)
1 can tomato soup, reduced-sodium
  (10 oz or 284 mL)
1 can baked beans in tomato sauce
  (14 oz or 398 mL)
1 can mixed beans (19 oz or 540 mL)
  (kidney, garbanzo, combinations vary)
Sun-dried tomatoes (from a jar)
Madras curry paste
Soy sauce, reduced-sodium
Chunky salsa
Ketchup & Mustard
Salad dressing, poppy seed, light, or favorite
Salad dressing, fat-free (I like Vidalia onion)
Ranch dressing, fat-free (for dipping Veggies)
Lemon juice
Liquid honey

FROZEN FOODS

Baby carrots (1 cup)
Corn (1 cup)

BAKERY

Whole-wheat dinner rolls (6-8) (optional for Chili)
Bread crumbs, large (2 cups)
Pizza base, thin-crust, 12 inch

Custom Grocery List

RECIPE NAME   Page

_____

_____

_____

_____

_____

MEATS

DAIRY

PRODUCE

DRY ESSENTIALS

SPICES

BAKING GOODS

HELPERS

FROZEN FOODS

BAKERY

OTHER

MEATS

Chicken breasts, boneless, skinless (8) for 2 meals
   (2 1/2 lbs or 1125 g)
Pork loin chops, thick, boneless, trimmed (3)
   (1 lb or 450 g)
Racks of lamb, trimmed (2 racks), 16 ribs
   (1 1/2 lbs or 675 g)

DAIRY

Butter
Eggs (2)
Feta cheese, light (10 oz or 300 g)
Parmesan cheese, light, grated (3/4 cup)
Mozzarella cheese, part-skim, shredded (1 1/2 cups)

PRODUCE

Fresh garlic (from a jar)
Fresh ginger (from a jar)
Red onion (1)
Celery ribs (4)
Baby carrots (1 cup)
Leeks (2)
Grape tomatoes (1 cup)
Tomato, Roma (1)
English cucumber (1)
Corn on the cob (4-6 ears) or use frozen
Red bell pepper (1)
Green bell pepper (1)
Mushrooms (15) for 2 meals
Asparagus spears (20)
Bean sprouts (optional for Tuna Wontons)
Coleslaw mix, 4 cups (8 oz or 225 g)
   (I like the colorful one with carrots)
Spinach leaves, 1 bag (12 oz or 350 g)
Cilantro (optional for Couscous and Tuna Wontons)
Wonton wrappers, 3 1/2 square inches (24)
   (found in produce or dairy section)

OTHER

Heavy aluminum foil

SPICES

Basil leaves
Curry powder
Dill, dried (or use 1/2 cup fresh)
Mrs. Dash Original seasoning
Parsley flakes
Thyme leaves
Salt & Pepper

BAKING GOODS

Cooking spray
Olive oil, extra-virgin
Sesame oil
Peanut oil
Balsamic vinegar
Peanuts, unsalted, for two meals (can use almonds)

HELPERS

1 can chicken broth, reduced-sodium
   (10 oz or 284 mL)
1 can cream of mushroom soup
   (10 oz or 284 mL)
1 can pasta sauce (24 oz or 680 mL)
2 cans solid tuna in water (6 1/2 oz or 184 g each)
Salsa
Sambal Oelek (crushed chili paste)
Kepac Manis (sweet Indonesian soy sauce)
Italian dressing, light
Salad dressing, fat-free, your favorite
1 can pineapple chunks, unsweetened
   (14 oz or 398 mL)
Lime juice
Apricot jam
Liquid honey

FROZEN FOODS

Phyllo pastry (4 sheets)
Green beans (1 lb or 450 g)

DRY ESSENTIALS

Penne pasta (3/4 lb or 350 g)
Whole-wheat couscous (1 cup)
Basmati or white rice (1 1/2 cups)
Croutons

INDICES

Main Component

beef, chicken, pork, seafood, vegetarian

'cause you have an idea
of what you'd like

Prep Code

by color
for when timing is everything

Fat Content

from lowest to highest

'cause your health requires you
to watch your fat intake

Index by Main Component

Index by Main Component

Make It Vegetarian
(see About the Recipes pages for details)

Index by Prep Code

Index by Fat Content

Our Team

God - no picture on file

God has overseen our project since before we knew about it. In fact, he knew Ron and I were meant to be together, and together we would help families fix dinner, one family at a time! Thank you, God, for loving me despite the fact that I can be a turkey at times. Thanks for showing us to trust in being used for your purpose, of helping the family unit reduce stress in the home and be healthy!

Photography - Lisa Fryklund

Lisa continues to impress in our second book together. She is the Director of Photography for our show *Fixing Dinner* on Food Network. During principal photography of the show, she would lay down the movie camera and pick up the digital without skipping a beat, taking photos for the network. We were so impressed that we asked her to do the photography for our last two books. We can't believe the talent that girl has! Lisa has become a dear friend over the years as well, which tells a person a lot about her character, having to put up with me day in and day out! Lisa is an award-winning cinematographer with a wide range of experience. She has traveled the world filming for Discovery, TLC, CBC, ABC, History, CMT, HGTV and National Geographic, and that's just a few on a long list of projects she's undertaken.
Lisa Fryklund is the owner of her own company.
Fryklund Cinematography www.fryklund.com

Illustrations - Hermann Brandt

Once again Hermann joins our team. What I love about having him (other than that he is a great illustrator) is that he gets it; I mean he really gets it!!! After he draws a few comps for me after conferring and then reading the matching written work, we get into these long philosophical conversations about how important the family is and what we can do to save the world from the dinner dilemma! It's pretty cool!
Hermann studied art at the Pretoria Technicon Arts School in South Africa and is the owner of his own company.
Brandt Fine Art and Illustration

Assistant and Research - Glen Paton

Well girl, you helped me out three years ago and we've been working together ever since. Thanks for laughing with me through the crazy deadlines and ever-evolving job! Love you more!

Our Team

**Graphic Design and Almost Everything Else -
Ron Richard**
Book number five, honey, can you believe it?
Ron runs the day-to-day operations of our company and is
the graphic designer for our books. Sometimes I don't know
how he swings it all. I do know I love him and that we are
the best team ever! Husband, friend and boss with benefits!
He's also the financial planner, money creator (seriously...I
think he can do that sometimes), office manager, technical
support provider, contract negotiator, food stylist and editor.
Ron Richard is the co-owner (with me) of our own company.
Cooking for the Rushed Inc.
www.cookingfortherushed.com

Graphic Support - Kris Nielson
Kris joins us once again. How many people are as blessed as we are to have
a pro like this almost at our back door? And he's nice, too! Kris, you are such
an easy person to work with. Thanks for making us look so good! Kris is an
international award-winning graphic artist as well as a published author, pho-
tographer and a certified outdoor instructor and guide.
Kris Nielson is the principal designer of his own company.
Kris Nielson Design www.krisdesign.ca

Dietitian, Diabetes Consultant - Sandra Burgess B.A.Sc., R.D., C.D.E.
Sandra is an enthusiastic member of our team for a second time! She calculated all the food exchange and food group values. Her work revolves around
making diabetes something people can manage easily. She is an avid volun-
teer with the Canadian Diabetes Association and Inn from the Cold Society.
Sandra Burgess is a registered dietitian and a certified diabetes educator with
30 years of professional experience.

Editors, Test Families, Friends
What would we do without them?
A special thanks to our church family and our friends
who tested recipes, gave us feedback and encouraged us.
God Bless.

A Note from Sandi

As I evolve as a meal planner and as a writer, some goals change and some stay the same. One of my idealistic views was to publish our first book in 1999 and then every family on the planet would discover that I had spent years developing a plan that would work for them.

Ron and I tested 160 servings per week over a five-year period so that we had a really clear idea of what The Family ate during the workweek. After four bestselling books and our show *Fixing Dinner* on Food Network, I have to say, we feel more driven to help families now than we ever have before.

The following event was one of those times that reinforced how important family time really is. The number-one thing kids really want!

At the turn of the last century, we wanted to do something special for our kids...so we bribed the older teens to stay home with an undisclosed prize at the end. All we said was, "We won't force you to spend New Year's Eve with us; we will tell you however that whoever stays won't regret it." It drove them crazy, so they all stayed. We figured...why not bribe? How many times does a family get to spend the turn of a century together? We wanted to be with them!

We have seven kids, so you can imagine the monthly bills. Our kids were not handed money freely. They all had part-time jobs as soon as they could work. They got the basics and a few extras. We thought of taking the kids to a favorite ski resort close to where we live and staying in the hotel. For all of us to stay for the night was $2,000! Ron and I decided that we would take the $2,000 hotel cost we were considering and give it to the kids to spend on whatever they wanted.

All week we asked each one what they would like for an appetizer. Each night Ron and I made an appetizer and froze whatever we made. We cleaned the house as if the most special guests in the world were coming.

We planned 10 activities. The first was to build the Millennium Bridge from one century to another with Lego. (You can just imagine how much Lego we accumulated over the years.) They automatically got points for participation. Twenty dollars was paid out, in Monopoly money, for each of the 10 activities. Appetizer eating was one of the activities. Celebrating the midnight hour was one. One activity was each of our kids drew an envelope from a hat that had one of their brother's or sister's names on it. The envelope contained a blank piece of paper and a pen inside. They had to interview and write down the qualities each sibling thought the person on the envelope had. Once all the interviews were done, the interviewer had to seal the envelope with the comments inside and put the sealed envelope on that person's pillow. Each person could not read the comments until they were in bed.

This may sound silly, but one luxury our kids have never known is to have a magazine subscription. It's something they have always wanted. Soooo, just before bed there was a treasure hunt. The treasure at the end of the hunt was a copy of each of their favorite magazines. They were ecstatic! We all gathered at the kitchen table to count their dollars with them. Ron and I told them how proud we were of them for looking like they actually enjoyed the evening. They explained that they actually did and thanked us for the effort we had given to making the night unique. We broke the news to them that they not only got the magazine, but we had ordered each one of them a year's subscription. They were sooo excited and said that that was an awesome prize and threw in their Monopoly money. We said, "Why are you tossing in your Monopoly money?" They thought the magazine subscription was the prize! We said, "Yes, but that's for the treasure hunt." They quickly snatched back their money and asked, "There's more?" We doled out a real $20 bill for every $20 in Monopoly money they had. They couldn't believe their eyes. Each one of them got $200 to spend. We said, "Tomorrow is part of the prize too. You can decide where you would like to go for a family dinner. We are also taking you to a mall so you can spend your money." There was screaming, hooting and hollering.

They were all dying to get to their beds to read their envelopes. The next thing we knew there were kids walking from one room to another for hours, talking, laughing, hugging. What a memorable night for me! I think to this very day, the people who got the most out of that night were Ron and me. There was no TV except for the countdown from the Big Apple…had to do that! There were no movies, phones, distractions—just great food and ridiculous activities with our kids.

Every family has issues, including ours, but if we (as a society) can move forward in understanding that dinner time can be one of the most significant things we can do as a family—so many other things will fall right into place.